UNOFFICIAL

Harry Potter
Cookbook

A Culinary Adventure With 90 Magical Recipes
For Wizards and Non-Wizards

Jimmy Black

Table of Content

Introduction

There are many wonders in the world of wizardry. However, very few of them can be enjoyed by wizards and non-wizards alike. The kitchen is where these two worlds meet and allow one to have a taste of the other. Food shares the magic of both worlds and can be enjoyed on multiple occasions.

Rowling has portrayed the important role that food plays in Harry's life within her seven novels, be it breakfast, lunch, dinner, snacks or even a fun drink. The image of life at Hogwarts is brought to life with these bits of detail and is especially true for an American reader that is unfamiliar with the traditional menu of British meals. Foods like crumpets, spotted Dick, black pudding, and steak and kidney pie are some of the dishes most people from our side of the pond are less likely to come across in everyday life.

Magic in the Kitchen

Creating the different dishes inspired by the wizarding world is ideal for bringing a little magic to your dinner table. With this book, even non-wizard folk can conjure up something wonderful and delicious in an instant. Instead of waving a wand, you will be equipped with choice kitchen utensils and some powerful recipes. In these pages are the secret to conjuring up delicious treats, wonderous dishes, and delectable potions, plus so much more. For anyone not familiar with British cuisine, foods in the young wizard series may seem just that, foreign, but it plays an important part in the UK island culture with a rich historical past and fascinating beginnings.

Before we jump into the first of many delicious dishes, here are some tips:

1. Always be sure to start with a clean work station.

2. Read through the recipes and instructions carefully to make sure you have all the tools and ingredients you need before you start. If you don't believe you have the skill set for a recipe, don't feel disheartened. Remember: practice makes perfect (swish and flick)!

3. Please be aware that some of these recipes require high boiling heat and sharp cutting, so they might be harmful to children and should only be attempted by an adult.

4. Some recipes include ingredients that can be substituted for scarcity or an allergy. For currants, you can use dried cranberries. Vegetable oil can be replaced by canola oil.

5. Tempering egg yolks is the process of bringing the yolks up to a higher temperature slowly to prevent them from curdling, which is required in some recipes.

6. Make sure that ingredients like butter, eggs and milk are at room temperature when making cakes and cookies to avoid curdling.

7. Remember, if you are using glass pans or dark metal pans when baking cakes, lower the temperature by twenty-five degrees; As these pans hold heat much longer and become hotter.

CHAPTER I

Getting Sorted

Whether it is the beginning of the year or the end of term, there is never a dull meal served in the Great Hall. For a young wizard, being accepted into Hogwarts and getting sorted into a house at the start of their first year is like a rite of passage. So in true first-year fashion, we start off with the sorting ceremony. Most notably, we have the start-of-term feast. This happens during the sorting ceremony, where each first year is placed into a house of their own. The Sorting Hat places the witch or wizard into the house they are specifically suited for. May it be Gryffindor, Slytherin, Hufflepuff or Ravenclaw; everyone has a place where they belong. Unfortunately, not all of us have a staff of house-elves in the kitchen able to prepare magical meals for us, but with a few ingredients, the right equipment and some easy to follow directions, we can make our own delicious foods right here at home!

Harry has known very few delicious and unrestricted meals during his stay in the non-magical world. Though the Dursleys did not entirely starve Harry, they also did not allow him to indulge in the delectable meals that they enjoyed, much less allowed him to eat as much as he would have liked. This is why his first encounter with the enormous amounts of food and drink is such a significant experience for him.

The Great Hall is known for its amazing feasts and meals that students and staff enjoy from breakfast to dinner. Food is one of the few places the wizarding world can seamlessly meet the non-magical world, and non-wizard folk can enjoy the special recipes of their magical counterparts. To pay tribute at the beginning of a new school year and being sorted into a house, we start off with foods that represent the start of a new day, breakfast. We will also look at foods that focus on the different "flavours" of each house and what each house may hold! Please remember always to have an adult present to supervise these recipes!

How It Starts

The English breakfast is a dish that is composed of numerous different ingredients like back bacon, eggs, British sausage, baked beans, fried tomato, fried mushrooms, black pudding, and fried and toasted bread. These components vary depending on where you are located in Great Britain. The Scottish variation would include potato scones, haggis, and oatcakes. The Welsh might add some laver bread or cakes and maybe even some Penclawdd cockles. The Irish version would consist of white pudding, Irish soda bread, and Irish potato cakes. This meal would also traditionally include food items like pork cracklings, massive pork chops, and pork cracklings. Baked beans are also always homemade. Eggs here are cooked in various ways, but mainly fried, which is why this dish is casually known as the fry-up. It is usually enjoyed with tea, but coffee and freshly squeezed orange juice might also be included.

Historically, British breakfast is dated back to the early 1300s and was originally started by the English gentry who were determined to preserve the traditional English country lifestyle and the meals that came along with it. They used breakfast to showcase the variety of produce from their estates, thereby displaying their wealth. The social class of the gentry was in decline during the Victorian era, which led to the rise of merchants, industrialists, and businessmen. Because the Victorians idolized the gentry, they took on many of their habits and traditions and also refined and standardized the ingredients of the full English breakfast that we know today. This dish also became a staple component during the Industrial Revolution among the working classes. The peak of its popularity being during the 1950s where fifty percent of Britain started their day off with this dish. The first recipe appeared in 1840, and the ingredients would differ in various recipes.

Lightning Bolt Toast

Whether you are a first-year student or in your final year at Hogwarts, you are not oblivious to the lightning bolt scar that adorns the forehead of *The Chosen One*. What better way to pay tribute to Harry, than shaping your toast to match his scar.

Servings: 24

Prep Time: 30 minutes

Cook Time: 30-45 minutes

Ingredients:

- 1 ½ tbsp active dry yeast

- ½ cup white sugar

- 2 cups of warm water (around 110 degrees F)

- 1 ½ tsp of salt

- ¼ cup of vegetable oil (or Canola oil)

- 5-6 cups of all-purpose flour (or bread flour)

- Butter

Instructions:

1. Dissolve sugar in warm water using a large bowl and stir in the yeast. Allow it to proof for about five minutes until the yeast looks like a creamy foam.

2. Add oil and salt into the yeast and mix it.

3. Add in flour. Remember not to do this all at once, but one cup at a time.

4. Knead the dough for seven minutes and place it into a well-oiled bowl. Turn the dough to coat it in the oil. Cover the bowl with a damp cloth and leave the dough to rest for about an hour. This will allow the dough to double in size.

5. Punch your dough down and knead it for one minute. Divide in half and shape the halves into loaves.

6. Place your loaves into two greased pans and allow them to rise for thirty minutes or until they have risen an inch above the pans.

7. Bake the loaves at 350 degrees F for 30-40 minutes.

8. Place onto the cooling rack and allow them to cool.

9. After the bread has cooled, use your serrated knife to cut it. Place the slices into the toaster until they are the desired amount of crisp (depending on preference).

10. Use your lightning bolt cookie cutter to cut the toast into shape and spread a layer of butter over the bread. Serve warm!

Homemade Bangers

No English breakfast is really complete without a well-made British sausage. Of course, these can be bought, but traditionally all the ingredients to this iconic breakfast were homemade. Not to mention the bragging rights to having made your own bangers for your guests to enjoy! Keeping in mind that a meat grinder is not always a feature in most kitchens, you can substitute this tool with a food processor. If casings or a sausage stuffer is not available, don't fret! You can still create the sausages by portioning the ground meat into your preferred size, roll them with your hands into the desired length and shape, and then wrap them in food quality plastic wrap.

Servings: 20

Prep Time: 1 hour 30 minutes prep time, 30 minutes chill time (best results if chilled overnight)

Cook Time: 30 minutes

Ingredients:

• 4 lbs boneless pork shoulder cut into ½-inch pieces and placed in a freezer for 45 minutes before it gets ground up

• 1 lb pork back fat cut into ½-inch pieces and placed in a freezer for 45 minutes before grinding

• 1 cup crushed ice

• 2 to 2 ½ cups ice-cold water

• 1 cup of coarse homemade bread crumbs from twice toasted bread (Note: This is very important for traditional banger texture and flavour. Don't use the premade bread crumbs from the store.)

• 2 ½ tbsp of salt

- 1 ½ tbsp of freshly ground white pepper

- 1 ½ tbsp of minced fresh sage

- 2 tsp of onion powder

- 2 tsp of ground ginger

- 2 tsp of ground mace (or substitute for additional nutmeg)

- 1 tsp of ground nutmeg

- 32mm natural hog casing, 15-20 feet soaked in warm water and thoroughly rinsed

Instructions:

1. Combine the pork, fat and crushed ice in a bowl. While working quickly, use a meat grinder to grind the mixture through a medium die.

2. Put the mixture in the freezer for 30 minutes and then grind again through a small die. Please note that it is important that the meat is kept at a cold temperature, so the fat does not become too soft. The lean meat and specs of fat must be clearly visible in the ground mixture.

3. Place ground meat in the bowl of a stand mixer fitted with a paddle attachment.

4. Add all the remaining ingredients except for the hog casings.

5. Mix the meat with the paddle for three to four minutes until threads begin to appear in the meat (the meat will create tiny threads when you pull it apart). This will indicate that your meat is ready. Add more ice water if the mixture is dry and stiff. You need the mixture to be smooth to go into the casings easily. During this process, you also need to taste the mixture to check the seasoning.

6. Take a small piece and fry it. Taste and add seasoning to the mixture if needed.

7. Put the mixture into the fridge to chill while you are preparing the casings.

8. Thread your sausage stuffer with the prepared hog casings, and then fill the sausage stuffer with the meat mixture. While being careful to avoid air gaps, stuff the casing. Be careful not to over-stuff.

9. Twist the sausages into links, and using a sausage pricker, prick any air bubbles out of the links.

10. Leave the sausages overnight to chill for the best results, as this allows the flavours to develop.

11. Cook the sausages by gently poaching them in slightly salted water and then grill or fry them. Note that if they are poached, they can be refrigerated for a week if tightly wrapped.

Not-So Every Flavor Baked Beans

Baked beans are mostly store-bought, and for convenience, usually come in a can. However, they are normally homemade for an English breakfast. The house-elves at Hogwarts don't always have access to muggle conveniences, having to make large batches to serve to the students. But you can do it with no problem with this simple yummy recipe.

Servings: 6

Prep Time: 24 hours (overnight soak)

Cook Time: 7 hours

Ingredients:

- 2 cups navy or white beans

- ½ lb bacon

- 1 onion, finely diced

- 3 tbsp molasses

- 2 tsp salt

- ¼ tsp ground black pepper

- ¼ tsp dry mustard

- ½ cup ketchup

- 1 tbsp Worcestershire sauce

- ¼ cup brown sugar

Instructions:

1. Soak the beans overnight in cold water.

2. Simmer in the same water until tender for one to two hours. Drain and reserve the liquid.

3. Preheat the oven to 325 degrees F.

4. Arrange the beans in a casserole dish by placing a section of the beans in the bottom of the dish and layering them with bacon and onions.

5. Combine molasses, salt, pepper, dry mustard, ketchup, Worcestershire sauce, and brown sugar in a saucepan and bring the mixture to a boil. Pour the mixture over the beans. Then pour in the reserved bean water, just enough to submerge the beans and cover the dish with a lid or aluminum foil.

6. Bake the beans for three to four hours in the oven until tender. Remove the lid about halfway through cooking, adding more liquid if needed to keep the beans from drying out too much.

Black Lake Pudding

Black pudding is not everyone's cup of tea, so to speak. This is because the ingredients may be a bit frightening for the squeamish eater. This can be a delicious flavour to try for a non-Brit foodie.

Servings: about 3 lbs

Prep Time: 30 minutes

Cook Time: 1 hour 30 minutes

Ingredients:

- 4 cups fresh pig's blood or powdered

- 2 ½ tsp salt

- 1 ½ cups steel-cut (pinhead) oatmeal

- 2 cups finely diced pork fat (or beef suet), finely chopped

- 1 large yellow onion, finely chopped

- 1 cup milk

- 1 ½ tsp freshly ground black pepper

- 1 tsp ground allspice

Instructions:

1. Preheat the oven to 325 degrees F and grease two glass loaf pans. Stir 1 teaspoon of salt into the blood.

2. Bring 2 ½ cups water to a boil and stir in the oats. Simmer, occasionally stirring, for fifteen minutes until it is tender, but avoid it getting mushy.

3. Pour the blood through a fine colander into a large bowl to remove any lumps.

4. Stir in the fat, onion, milk, pepper, allspice, and rest of the salt. Then add in the oatmeal and mix it together.

5. Divide the mixture between the loaf pans and cover them with foil. Bake for one hour until firm. Allow it to cool completely and seal it in plastic wrap. Freeze-dry it for prolonged use or store it in the fridge for up to a week.

6. Cut a slice of about 1/2-inch thick off the loaf and fry it in butter or oil until the edges are lightly crisped and browned before serving.

Grand Fry-Up Feast

We don't always have a lot of time or ability to create a complete home-made meal, and unfortunately, we can't wave a wand or cast a spell to get the job done for us. We do, however, have premade ingredients! This is a little magic that we, as non-wizards, can use to still enjoy a delicious dish.

Servings: 1

Prep Time: 5-10 minutes

Cook Time: 30 minutes

Ingredients:

- 2 pork sausages

- 1 tomato

- 2 tbsp butter

- 2 rashers bacon

- 3.9 oz mushrooms

- 1 (7.8 oz) can baked beans

- 1 large egg

- 2 slices white or brown bread

- salt and pepper to taste

- 1 sprig parsley

Instructions:

1. Preheat the oven to 430 degrees F.

2. Place a pan over medium heat, and when hot brown your sausages on all sides. Cook for five minutes, then place them into a baking dish and bake them for ten minutes in the oven.

3. Using a knife, cut a cross on the bottom of the tomato and place it in the baking dish with the sausages, facing the cross side up. Bake the tomato with the sausages for ten minutes, then switch off the heat and leave in the oven to stay warm.

4. In the same frying pan that you fried the sausages, melt a tablespoon of butter and add in the mushrooms and bacon. Fry them over high heat for seven minutes until the mushrooms have turned soft and the bacon crispy. Move to the oven to keep them warm.

5. Add the beans to a small saucepan and cook them over medium heat, stirring constantly.

6. Finally, fry the egg, making sure the yolk stays intact and toast the bread. Spread the leftover butter over the toast.

7. Arrange the ingredients on a warm plate and season them with salt and pepper. Enjoy!

Hocus Pocus Fizz (Alcoholic)

Breakfast would not be complete without orange juice, especially one with a kick like this one. This drink is made with alcohol but can be substituted with sparkling cider for kids to enjoy.

Servings: 6

Prep Time: 5 minutes

Cook Time: 0 minutes

Ingredients:

- 3 drops red food colouring

- 2 drops yellow food colouring

- ¼ tsp coconut extract

- 1 cup pineapple juice

- ½ cup rum, white (optional)

- 1 bottle sparkling white wine (substitute sparkling grape juice or cider for non-alcoholic option)

- Ice

Instructions:

1. Mix the pineapple juice, coconut extract, white rum.

2. Add in red and yellow food colouring for a fun orange tint.

3. Shake or mix with a spoon before adding sparkling wine to fill.

4. Serve over ice.

Sorting Hat Cheese Balls

Servings: 30

Prep Time: 3 hours and 30 minutes

Cook Time: 0 minutes

Ingredients:

- 2 (8 oz) packages cream cheese, softened

- ½ cup (1 stick) butter, softened

- 2.5 cups shredded cheddar cheese

- 1 (0.7 oz) package Italian salad dressing mix

- ¼ cup poppy seeds

- Veggies or crackers

Instructions:

1. Combine the cream cheese, butter, cheese, and dressing mix in a stand mixer and mix on medium until well combined.

2. Shape a third of the cheese mixture into a six-inch diameter disc shape to create the brim of the hat.

3. Form the rest of the cheese mixture into a cone shape. This will be the top part of the hat.

4. Cover both shapes in plastic wrap, then place it into the fridge for at least one hour.

5. Take the shapes out of the fridge, place the cone on top of the disc, and place it on top of the disc on your serving platter and blend them

together. Shape the facial features into the cone and bend the point back slightly to define the sorting hat in a bit more detail.

6. Press the poppy seeds into the surface of the cheese hat until you have completely covered it. The easiest way to do this is by sprinkling the seeds into your palms and gently pressing them on the larger sections. This will get a little messy, so to avoid a tedious cleanup, place a cloth underneath it.

7. Gently wrap the plastic wrap around the cheese ball hat and place it into the refrigerator for at least two hours. Do this the day before and leave it overnight.

8. Take it out of the fridge thirty minutes before serving with your favourite vegetables or crackers.

Babbling Charm Stuffed Burgers

Servings: 6

Prep Time: 30-45 minutes

Cook Time: 10-15 minutes for the patties, 15-20 minutes for buns

Ingredients:

Buns

- ½ cup of water

- 1 tsp dried yeast

- 1 ½ tsp milk

- 1 ½ cups of strong white bread flour

- 1 tbsp caster sugar

- ½ tsp salt

- 2 tbsp unsalted butter

- 1 egg

- Extra egg and splash of milk for egg-wash

Stuffed Burger

- 1 pound of preferred beef

- 1 egg

- 1 tsp Worcestershire sauce

- salt and pepper to taste

- 1 tsp paprika

- 3 cloves garlic

- 1 onion

- ½ cup mozzarella cheese

- ½ cup cheddar cheese

- 3 ½ tbsp double cream

- red, yellow, blue, and green food colouring gel

Toppings

- 5-6 lettuce leaves

- 1 tomato

- 1 pickle

- ¼ onion

Instructions:

1. Start preparing buns by warming the milk and water. Add yeast to the liquids and pour the mixture into a bowl. Whisk and set aside for ten minutes to allow the yeast to activate. The mixture will be very bubbly when it's ready.

2. Add the flour, salt, and sugar to the bowl and combine by stirring thoroughly, then add in the butter. To form fine bread crumbs, work the butter into the flour and then create a well in the middle.

3. Break the egg into a jug and whisk it well before pouring it into the well with the yeast mixture. For five to ten minutes, knead the dough together until the texture becomes soft and springy and shape it into a ball.

4. Grease the bowl lightly with oil, and place the dough in. Cover the dough with plastic wrap and allow it to rise for an hour or until it has doubled in size.

5. To get the cheese ready, put a saucepan on low to medium heat and add in both mozzarella, cheddar, and cream cheese. Keep stirring the mixture until everything is melted.

6. Divide the cheese mixture into four separate bowls and add the food colouring to each bowl to represent the different Hogwarts houses. With a spoon, place the mixture into an ice tray and put it into the fridge to set.

7. Check the dough you prepared earlier to see if it has risen and knock back the air a little bit by kneading it for a minute. Place the dough onto a lightly floured surface and knead it quickly. Then roll the dough down until about an inch thick and cut into rounds using a cookie cutter.

8. Put the rounds into your oiled bun moulds (or folded tin foil if you don't have moulds) and cover it with plastic wrap to allow the dough to rise and double in size again.

9. To prepare the patty, grate the onion and crush the garlic before adding it to the bowl of ground beef. Use salt and pepper to add flavour, as well as the Worcestershire sauce and paprika.

10. After you add the spices, add in the egg, work the ground beef mixture well, combine all the ingredients, and be careful not to over mix it.

11. Divide the beef into six balls and flatten.

12. Take out the cheese from the fridge and place one or two cubes into the middle of each patty. Fold the sides over into the middle to keep the cheese in place and make sure it is well sealed.

13. When the buns are ready, whisk the egg and milk together to create an egg wash and brush it over the buns.

14. Bake in the oven for 15-20 minutes at 350 degrees F or until it has risen and turned golden brown.

15. During this time, you can start frying the burger patties. Place a saucepan on medium heat with a little bit of oil and begin to fry your burgers a couple at a time for about 4-5 minutes, then flip the burgers and fry for another 5 minutes. If you want the center to stay melted, keep them in a warm oven while you complete the recipe.

16. Take the buns out of the moulds, and with a serrated knife, slice it in half. Place your burger patties onto the buns and add your toppings. Serve with your favourite sauces!

4-Flavor Homemade Pota-
to and Root Veggie Chips

Every house has distinctive traits and flavours that set them apart from each other. Translating those traits to seasoning, this will be sure to tickle the palette of your magical and non-magical friends and will allow them to have a taste of each.

Servings: 4

Prep Time: 15-20 minutes

Cook Time: 10-15 minutes

Ingredients:

Potato chips

- 1.5 lbs low-sugar potatoes (Carisma potatoes or yams)

- oil for frying

Root vegetable chips

- 1 sweet potato

- 2 beetroots

- 1 parsnip

- 1 carrot

Seasoning

- maltodextrin

- salt

- 2 oz chorizo

- 1 red pepper

- 1 lime

- black pepper

- 1 tbsp honey

- 1 tbsp wholegrain mustard

Instructions:

1. Prepare your potatoes by peeling and washing them, then leave them in a bowl of water to keep them from turning brown.

2. Slice the potatoes as thinly as you can. You can use a food processor, knife, or grater. Place the thin slices between a paper towel to remove any extra water. Repeat these steps on your root vegetables.

3. Making the seasoning, you use maltodextrin to assist with absorbing the flavours from the ingredients. This keeps them in a powder form that can be sprinkled over the chips.

4. Starting off with Gryffindor, cut the chorizo and red peppers into chunks and roast them in the oven at 350 degrees F for twenty minutes.

5. After taking the chunks out of the oven, place them in a food processor and blend them. Add in four to five tablespoons of maltodextrin into a bowl, adding in the puree, a little bit at a time. Whisk it together as quickly as you can to avoid any clumps.

6. When the maltodextrin becomes lightly coloured, making sure it is still powdered, press it through a sieve to remove any clumps.

7. Add salt to the powder.

8. Separately, prepare the Slytherin flavouring by squeezing the juice from the limes and add it into four to five tablespoons of maltodextrin. Whisk it together slowly.

9. Press the powder through a sieve to remove any clumps and add salt and pepper.

10. Next up is Hufflepuff. Mix the honey and mustard together in a bowl and add it to four to five tablespoons of maltodextrin, do this in drops and not all together.

11. Whisk it through the powder and press through a sieve. Add salt to the powder.

12. Pour some oil into a pan and place it on high heat of about 350 degrees F.

13. For two to three minutes, fry your potato slices in batches, making sure that you have enough space to turn them now and then.

14. When cooked, remove them from the oil and place them on some paper towels to remove the excess oil.

15. The root vegetable chips will be representing Ravenclaw and can also be fried in batches separately for three to four minutes.

16. Separate the white potato chips into three bowls and sprinkle them with the maltodextrin while they are still hot and a bit oily. Toss them together to spread the powdered seasoning.

17. Add salt to the root vegetables.

18. Store any leftover chips in an air-tight container.

Confringo Chocolate Cupcakes

Servings: 12 medium cupcakes

Prep Time: 30-45 minutes

Cook Time: 10-15 minutes

Ingredients:

Cupcakes

- 4 oz golden caster sugar

- 4 oz butter

- 2 eggs

- 4 oz self-raising flour

- ½ tsp vanilla extract

- ¼ tsp ground mixed spice

- 2 tbsp cocoa powder

- 2 tbsp boiling water

- gold sprinkles

White Chocolate Buttercream

- 4 oz butter

- 8 oz icing sugar

- 1 tsp vanilla extract

- 1 tbsp milk

- 3.5 oz white chocolate

- Red, green, blue, and yellow food colouring

Instructions:

1. Cream together your butter and sugar until it is light and fluffy. Scrape the sides down and keep mixing it together for another minute.

2. Break the eggs into a jug, whisking them lightly and add slowly to the butter and sugar. Mix until smooth.

3. Add your vanilla and mixed spice into the bowl and make a paste out of cocoa powder and hot water. Add the cocoa paste into the mixture and mix it well until it becomes smooth. Whisk it together until the mix is just combined.

4. Line the cupcake tray with wrappers. Spoon the batter into the wrappers until they are just over half full. Level the batter out by tapping the tray gently.

5. Bake the cupcakes for 10-15 minutes. Use a skewer to check if they are done by poking the skewer through the middle of the cupcake. If it comes out clean, they are done.

6. Prepare the white chocolate buttercream while the cupcakes are cooling on a cooling tray. Melt the white chocolate in a bowl over simmering water (or in the microwave. Set it aside and allow it to cool.

7. Whisk the butter until smooth and add a third of the icing sugar, mixing it for one to two minutes and add another third of icing sugar. Repeat this step until all of the icing sugar is incorporated.

8. Use milk, vanilla, and the cooled white chocolate to flavour the buttercream. Whisk together for one to two minutes until it forms firm peaks.

9. Take out a third of the buttercream frosting for the centers and divide it into four bowls. Add a food dye to each bowl for house colours.

10. Using a spoon, create a hole in your cupcakes and fill them with one to two teaspoons of the coloured frosting.

11. Lastly, place the leftover buttercream into a piping bag with a star nozzle and pipe a swirl on top of the cupcake, ensuring that the coloured frosting in the middle is covered.

12. Decorate the cupcakes with golden sprinkles to add a bit of magic.

Sun-Dried Tomato and Basil Sorting Hat Rolls

Servings: 16

Prep Time: 25 minutes

Cook Time: 10-15 minutes

Ingredients:

- 2 tubes (8 oz each) refrigerated crescent rolls

- ¼ cup butter softened

- ¼ cup minced fresh basil

- 2 tbsp oil-packed sun-dried tomatoes, patted dry and finely chopped

- ½ tsp garlic powder

Instructions:

1. Preheat the oven to 375 degrees F.

2. Unroll each of the tubes of dough and separate each dough roll into eight triangles.

3. Using a small bowl, mix the garlic powder, sun-dried tomatoes, basil and softened butter together.

4. Spread a teaspoon of the filling along the wide end of each of the triangles and carefully roll up each triangle once to form the hat's brim.

5. Place the triangles separately on a greased baking sheet and bake for ten to twelve minutes, or until they turn golden brown. Turn them halfway to brown evenly.

Pumpkin Juice

Pumpkin juice is a big favourite of Harry's and his fellow wizards and witches. It accompanies almost every meal, and now you can make it too! This drink is perfect for breakfast, lunch, dinner, and anytime in between.

Servings: 16

Prep Time: 5 minutes

Cook Time: 0 minutes

Ingredients:

- 1 gallon of apple cider (or apple juice)

- 15 oz pumpkin puree

- ½ cup sugar

- ½ cup brown sugar

- 2 tsp pumpkin pie spice

- 2 tsp vanilla

- Ice

Instructions:

1. Mix all of the ingredients in a large pitcher, being sure to stir well.

2. Pour over ice in separate glasses.

3. Stir again before serving.

House Cup Marmalade

Marmalade is also one of the magical treats that can be enjoyed in the magical world and the non-magical folk's world. It is usually served with breakfast at Hogwarts, and it isn't hard to imagine that every house might have its own distinctive flavour.

Servings: 4 large jars

Prep Time: 1 hour

Cook Time: 45 minutes

Ingredients:

Lemon Marmalade - Hufflepuff

- 3 lemons (approx. 9 oz)

- 17 fl oz water

- 18 oz granulated sugar

Lime Marmalade - Slytherin

- 3 limes (approximately 9 oz)

- 17 fl oz water

- 18 oz granulated sugar

Beetroot Marmalade - Ravenclaw

- 2 pre-cooked beetroots

- 1 lemon

- 17 fl oz water

- 18 oz jam sugar

Pomegranate Marmalade - Gryffindor

- 1 large pomegranate

- 1 lemon

- 17 fl oz water

- 18 oz jam sugar

Note: Fruits with hard rinds need to be softened.

Instructions:

1. Place the lemons and limes into separate pots, add water and cover the pots.

2. Bring the water to a boil and let the lemons and limes simmer for 30-45 minutes until the fruits are soft.

3. Keep the liquid aside, removing fruit and letting them cool.

4. As soon as the fruit is cool enough to handle, cut the fruit and remove the pulp, placing it into a muslin cloth.

5. Tie the cloth and place it into the pot with your liquid. Leave the cloth entirely if you don't want the marmalade to be too bitter.

6. Slice the softened rinds thinly and add them into the pot with your sugar.

7. Stir it until the sugar has dissolved and put the mixture to a boil. Let boil rapidly for 10-15 minutes until the marmalade reaches its setting point at around 230 degrees F.

8. Remove any scum that may form at the top with a spoon to keep the marmalade clear.

9. Pour the marmalade into a heatproof jug and allow it to cool for a few minutes before pouring it over into sterilized jars.

10. Fruits low in pectin are normally rindless and don't need to be boiled first. To add flavour, put the beetroot into a muslin cloth with the cut lemon, tie and infuse by letting it simmer for five minutes. The same can be done with the pomegranate seeds in a different pot.

11. When they are infused, slice the beetroot thinly and place it into the pan with your infused water and jam sugar.

12. Bring the mixture to a boil for 10-15 minutes until it has reached its setting point.

13. Pour it into your jugs and allow it to cool for a few minutes before sealing the jar immediately.

14. Repeat this process for the pomegranate seeds. Add the seeds into a pot with the sugar and infused water. Bring to a boil for 10-15 minutes, place it in a jar and seal it before allowing it to cool.

House Butter

Servings: 4 (5-7 oz) blocks

Prep Time: 15-20 minutes

Cook Time: 45 minutes

Ingredients:

Unsalted Butter

- 40.5 fl oz double cream

Caramelized Onion Butter (Ravenclaw)

- ½ tsp salt flakes

- ½ red onion

- oil for frying

Garlic Butter (Slytherin)

- ½ tsp salt flakes

- 3 cloves garlic

- a handful of flat-leaf parsley

Peri Sun-Dried Tomato Butter (Gryffindor)

- ½ tsp salt

- ½ tsp peri-peri flakes

- 2-3 sun-dried tomatoes

Honey Mustard Butter (Hufflepuff)

- ½ tsp salt

- ½ tsp honey

- ½ tsp mustard

Instructions:

1. For an unsalted butter base, pour the double cream into a bowl and whisk on medium to high speed for five to ten minutes.

2. While you whisk, the mixture will start to become thicker and then split. Keep whisking, and the liquids and fat solids will separate.

3. Take out the solids from the bowl and, using a colander, strain.

4. Place it into a muslin cloth and squeeze it repeatedly to remove excess water. Take out the solids from the bowl and strain through a colander.

5. Divide the butter into four pieces and add the corresponding flavours.

6. Salt and caramelized onion for Ravenclaw. Salt, garlic and parsley for Slytherin. Peri flakes, salt and tomatoes are Gryffindor. Honey mustard for Hufflepuff. Mix the flavours through the butter mix until they are combined well.

7. Shape your butter into blocks using butter paddles or spatulas if you don't have the former ready. Smooth them over and chill each for thirty minutes.

8. Serve them as is or cut into lightning bolts for a unique display.

Ravenclaw

9. Prepare ingredients and allow them enough time to cool down and dry. Place a pan on medium heat and add your oil.

10. Slice the onion into strips and place it into the heated oil. Keep it moving to allow the onions to caramelize for 3-5 minutes.

11. If the onions begin to stick to the pan, add more oil.

12. When you are happy with the colour, remove the onions and drain them on a paper towel.

Slytherin

13. Remove the parsley from the stems and chop them up finely. Also, peel and press your garlic through a garlic crusher.

Gryffindor

14. Remove the tomatoes from the oil and chop them into small pieces. Press them between two paper towel pieces and remove the extra oil.

Flying Letter Cake

Cake is one of the most eagerly awaited party foods, just as is any young witch or wizard looking to be accepted into Hogwarts. This delicious recipe will be perfectly suited to transport your guests into the magical world. But be careful, this will fly off the plate!

Servings: 12-16

Prep Time: 25-30 minutes

Cook Time: 40-45 minutes

Ingredients:

Gryffindor Sponge Cake

- 20 oz butter

- 20 oz golden caster sugar

- 10 eggs

- 20 oz self-raising flour

- 1 tbsp vanilla extract

- ½ tbsp mixed spice

Vanilla Buttercream Filling

- 10 oz butter

- 20 oz icing sugar

- 1 tbsp vanilla extract

- 2 tbsp milk

- red food colouring

Royal Green Frosting

- 2 egg whites

- 12 oz icing sugar

- 1-2 tsp lemon juice

- green food colouring

Decorations

- 16 oz white fondant icing

- yellow and red food colouring

- 1 tbsp raspberry jam

- cocoa powder

Instructions:

1. Start your sponge cake by creaming butter and sugar together until it is light and fluffy.

2. Beat in your eggs one at a time while scraping off the sides of the bowl. Add in a spoonful of flour with each egg, as this will ensure they do not curdle, and the mixture will rise correctly when placed in the oven.

3. Add in the vanilla, mixed spice and the remaining flour and continue to mix through until it is properly combined.

4. Taking a third of this mixture, place it in a separate bowl and add your red food colouring. Keep stirring it through until you have a vibrant red colour distributed evenly.

5. Line and grease an eight-inch square baking tin and add your white and red cake batter one spoonful at a time, in different spots around the tin. Tap the tin gently against the counter to even it out and, using a skewer, marble the batter together. Don't overdo it, as it will continue to mix while it is baking.

6. Bake the cake at 350 degrees F in the oven for 40 minutes and until golden. Check the cake by inserting a skewer in the middle. If it is clean when you pull it out, the cake is done.

7. To make the buttercream, whisk the room temperature butter until it is nice and smooth, then add in the icing sugar one third at a time. Whisk them through each time you add the icing sugar until they are well combined.

8. Using vanilla and milk, flavour the buttercream, scraping down the sides and continuing to whisk for another minute until it is fluffy and light.

9. Divide the icing into two and add red dye to half of the buttercream. Place the red buttercream into a separate piping bag from the white buttercream and put these aside until it is time to decorate.

10. Level the top of your cake, so it's nice and even and then create a stencil for your letters. Use this stencil to cut out your sponge. Cut your sponge cake horizontally to create two layers for you to sandwich together.

11. Using the white buttercream, pipe a border around the first layer of cake and then pipe diagonally, alternating with the red and white buttercream as you pipe along the middle.

12. Sandwich the next layer of cake on the top and carve the sponges down to give you three levels to your letter. This will give it a 3D effect.

13. Using white buttercream, add a crumb coat to the whole cake, ensuring not to lose any definition from your carving and place the cake in the fridge to set for an hour.

14. Using the yellow food dye, create the off-white envelope colour by kneading the dye into the fondant and allowing it to sit on one side so the colouring can settle. Repeat this process to create the wax seal using the red dye.

15. Put some frosting onto the surface and then roll out the white fondant to 0.2 inches thick. Then, using the rolling pin, lift the fondant over the cake and then smooth it over the top and sides.

16. Trim the sides, and using a fondant smoother, square off the sides and emphasize the definition of the letters.

17. Place the cake back in the fridge to set for a minimum of thirty minutes.

18. Roll out the red fondant roughly and then use a Hogwarts stamp cookie cutter to press into the middle. By pinching the edges, using your fingers, you can create a wax drip effect.

Icing

19. Pasteurize the egg whites in a bowl over hot water, whisking it, and then placing it into the mixing bowl until it is frothy and light.

20. Add in the icing sugar, a spoonful at a time, and once the mixture starts to leave trails that do not vanish for about ten seconds, the mixture is ready to go.

21. You can now add in the green food colouring and whisk it through.

22. Place it in a piping bag, using a writing tip.

23. With some hot water, thin your jam and brush it over your wax stamp. This will give it a melted and shiny look.

24. Then dab the cake with some of the cocoa powder and blend it to make the letter look aged. You can now also add in any of the other fondant indentations to the cake.

25. Be sure to practice piping your lettering onto some wax paper until you are confident. Then pipe the address on top of the letters.

26. Using the spare red buttercream, finish off by piping around the border of the cake and your cardboard.

CHAPTER II

The Express Train to Yummy Treats

The Hogwarts Express plays an important role in young Harry's life. He meets most of the young wizards and witches who play a large part in his experience at Hogwarts and his adventures. After all, this is where he meets his two closest friends Ron and Hermoine. The snacks he buys to share with Ron comes from the food trolley cart, where he buys "the lot," and tasting each of what the wizarding world had to offer in regards to fun candy and cakes. We might not have Honeydukes on every corner to experience the tasty treats, but we can try and make our own copycat candies in the recipes to follow.

Jelly Slugs

Servings: approximately 10-12 slugs

Prep Time: 4-6 hours

Cook Time: 5-10 minutes

Ingredients:

Blackberry Jelly Slugs

- 5 oz fresh blackberries

- 8 ½ oz water

- 1 tbsp golden caster sugar

- 6 gelatine leaves

- 27 oz sugar (for temporary mould and can be reused)

- 2 oz fondant

- a few cocktail sticks

Edible Slime

- 1 lemon (zest and juice)

- green food colouring

- 1 egg

- 2 oz caster sugar

- 1 ½ tbsp butter (room temperature)

Instructions:

1. Make the jelly gummy sweets by placing the blackberries, sugar, and water into a pan. Place this on medium heat and cook it for 5 minutes until the fruit is soft, and then place it into a food processor.

2. Blend the mixture until it's smooth, and then pass it through a sieve to press out as much of the juice as you can.

3. Bloom the gelatine by placing them into a bowl with some cold water and leaving them for five minutes. When they have softened, squeeze out the excess water and add the gelatine into the pan with the blackberry juice, stirring it until it has dissolved. Move it to a heatproof jug and leave it to cool entirely.

4. Add the sugar into a square baking tray at least half an inch deep and level it out with an offset spatula. Make your slugs by moulding the fondant into slug shapes, turn them upside down and leave them to harden for thirty minutes. Gently make your indents by pressing the slugs into the sugar.

5. Use a pipette to ease the jelly mixture into the slug moulds, placing them in the fridge to set for two to four hours.

6. During the time your jelly mixture is setting, you can start making your edible slime. Zest your lemon and juice it.

7. Place a bowl over a pan of simmering water, adding the lemon juice and zest, along with the green food colouring to the water. In a separate bowl, whisk an egg and sugar together until they are light and frothy, then slowly add the egg into the warm lemon juice while whisking continuously to keep lumps from forming.

8. Add in the butter and keep whisking until it is completely melted. Keep heating and mixing it for another five minutes, and you should notice it thickening up.

9. Take the slime off from the heat and cover with plastic wrap. Press the plastic wrap down to the surface of the slime to keep it from forming a skin.

10. As soon as the jelly slugs are set completely, take them out of the sugar and sprinkle it out thinly. Leave it out to dry for a few hours, and then sift the sugar and place it back into your bag to be used again as normal.

11. Dip the jelly slugs into your edible slime, coating them nice and evenly and then place them onto a serving dish. Add some slime trails to make them seem like they are moving.

Mars Bar

Servings: 6-8

Prep Time: 1 hour

Cook Time: 40 minutes

Ingredients:

Caramel

- 5 oz sugar

- 1 ½ fl oz water

- 2 tbsp glucose syrup (or corn syrup)

- pinch of salt

- 5 fl oz cream

Nougat

- 8 oz sugar

- 2 tbsp glucose syrup

- 1 ½ fl oz water

- 3 egg whites

- 1/2 tsp vanilla extract

- pinch of salt

- 3 ½ oz milk chocolate

Chocolate Toppings

- 7 oz milk chocolate

- 2 oz white chocolate (optional)

Instructions:

1. Begin making the chocolate nougat by placing a heavy-bottomed saucepan on medium heat. Then add in the sugar, water, and liquid glucose. Don't forget the salt! Mix the ingredients around in a swirling motion to help the sugar dissolve and bring it to a boil.

2. After two or three minutes of bubbling, when the sugar just starts to turn golden, pour in the double cream carefully and whisk it through until combined. Place a sugar thermometer and heat to the 'firm ball' stage at 250 degrees F.

3. Double line an 8-inch rectangular tin with plastic wrap and press it into the corners. Pour in the caramel and level it off by easing it into the corners with a spatula.

4. Now, you can go ahead and make a sugar syrup by adding sugar glucose and water into a pan and bringing it to a boil. Heat to 300 degrees F.

5. Separate the eggs and put the whites into a bowl, whisking them until soft peaks are formed.

6. Flavor the nougat with chocolate by melting the chocolate in a bowl over simmering water or microwave, stir until it becomes smooth.

7. Keep whisking the nougat slowly while slowly pouring in the sugar syrup in a thin stream. Once all the syrup has been blended, the hot sides of the bowl will become apparent. Keep whisking for 5-10 minutes while it is cooling down, and the nougat becomes thicker.

8. Add the vanilla, salt, and melted chocolate into the nougat and fold it through gently while being careful not to knock out too much air. Take the caramel out of the fridge and place the nougat on top of it. Make it even with a spatula and then return it to the fridge for thirty minutes to set.

9. Transfer the caramel and nougat to the freezer for another thirty minutes to ensure you are getting clean edges. Heat up a sharp knife with boiling water or a blow torch. Take the caramel nougat out of the tin and peel off the plastic wrap. Slice them into six to eight bars and return them to the fridge.

10. Using the half tempering method, place the chocolate into a bowl over simmering water and melt until it becomes smooth. Remove it from the heat once it has melted. This is to create a nice snap to it.

11. Chop the leftover chocolate into small chunks and add them to the melted chocolate a little bit at a time. Keep stirring until it's all melted, and then allow the mixture to cool down.

12. Dip the nougat base of each bar into the chocolate and put it onto a wire rack to let it set. Once they have set, flip them over and pour the remaining chocolate over them and over the sides. Using a skewer, swirl the pattern to the top.

13. (Optional) You can melt the extra white chocolate, and using a piping bag, pipe some lightning bolts on top. Pipe on some lightning bolts and place your bars back into the fridge and allow them to set.

Mint Humbug

Traditionally, this is a hard-boiled candy that is usually mint-flavoured and has an appearance of two different coloured stripes. It can usually be found in the United Kingdom, Ireland, South Africa, Canada, Australia, and New Zealand.

Servings: 20-30

Prep Time: 15-20 minutes

Cook Time: 10-15 minutes

Ingredients:

- 14 oz sugar

- ½ tsp cream of tartar

- 5.4 fl oz water

- 1 ½ tsp peppermint extract

- black food dye

Instructions:

1. Place a heavy-bottomed saucepan on high heat, then pour in your sugar, cream of tartar, water, and peppermint extract into the pan.

2. Swirl the mixture in the pan until the sugar has dissolved, don't over-mix it, however, as sugar crystals could form. Put in a sugar thermometer into the heat and heat up the mixture until it reaches 260 degrees F or the 'hard ball' stage.

3. When the sugar reaches the right temperature, take it off of the heat and leave to cool a little bit for 1-2 minutes.

4. The mixture should thicken slightly. This will allow you to pour it onto a silicone mat. You can make them two-toned by pouring two puddles onto the mat and only adding the food dye to one half.

5. Using a metal spatula, fold the outside of each sugar puddle into the center and repeat the process to create a firm ball.

6. Work each ball of candy using heatproof gloves by pulling and stretching it to blend in the air and let it thicken. The white candy mixtures should become cloudy and opaque.

7. The candy should be firm enough to hold its shape when left on the silicone mat after three to five minutes. Roll each of the colours into two sausages, then marble them together.

8. Keep rolling the marbled humbug mixture and then, using scissors, cut and mould them into the shapes you want. Remember to grease the scissors to keep them from sticking.

9. After you have moulded them into the shapes you want, let them cool completely. As soon as they have hardened, you can wrap them in either wax paper or cellophane and store them in an air-tight jar.

Pasteis de Nata

Servings: 24 custard tarts

Prep Time: 1 hour

Cook Time: 2 hours 30 minutes

Ingredients:

Pastry

- 14 oz plain flour

- ¼ tsp salt

- ¼ tsp cinnamon

- 7 fl oz cold water

- 8 oz butter (room temperature)

Egg Custard Filling

- 10 oz sugar

- 8 ½ oz water

- 1 cinnamon stick

- 5 oz double cream

- 5 oz milk

- 6 egg yolks

- 1 oz plain flour

- ½ tsp vanilla

Decoration

- 2 tbsp icing sugar

- 1 tbsp cinnamon

Instructions:

1. Start making the pastry by adding flour, salt, and cinnamon into a bowl. Mix it together and create a well in the middle. Pour the water into the middle of the well and mix it into the dough with a knife.

2. Knead the pastry on a lightly floured surface for a couple of minutes until it is smooth. Wrap in plastic wrap and place into the fridge for 15 minutes to relax the gluten strands and make them easier to work with.

3. Now, you can start making the custard filling while the pastry is chilling. Put the sugar, water and cinnamon stick into a pan over medium heat and let the mixture come to a boil at around 212 degrees F. When it is ready, take out the cinnamon stick and let the mixture cool.

4. Then, put your cream and milk into a pan, warm it while being careful not to burn. Add the egg yolks into a different bowl with the flour and vanilla as well. Whisk into a smooth paste.

5. Now, pour the cooled sugar syrup slowly into the eggs while continuously whisking the mixture to keep any lumps from forming. When it is appropriately combined, repeat the process with the warm milk and cream. Pour the egg custard through a sieve, removing any lumps and then letting it cool. To keep a skin from forming, cover the custard with plastic wrap.

6. Now, roll out the pastry into a rectangle, the pastry being about ¼ inch thick. Then take a third of your butter and spread it over two-thirds of the pastry. Leave an inch wide gap around the outside to keep the butter from spilling out.

7. Fold the unbuttered pastry over the middle, dust any excess flour off, and fold the remaining buttered section over the top. Press your rolling pin at the top and bottom to seal in place, rotate 90 degrees, and repeat, rolling into a larger rectangle and buttering with ⅓ more butter.

8. Fold and seal the dough, then roll it out into a rectangle, this time buttering the entire pastry evenly. Now roll the longest edge that is furthest away towards you, getting a tight roll as you go. Cut it into two pieces and wrap it in plastic to refrigerate for at least 4 hours or overnight.

9. Take out one of the pastry halves and slice it into twelve-inch wide circles. Then place it into a lightly greased muffin pan. Allow it to soften for ten minutes. Press the pastry towards the bottom with your fingers, wetting them before you do so, and then thinly coating the sides and bot-

tom so that it still sticks out from the top. You can also pour the cooled egg custard into each tart.

10. Bake the pastry in the oven at 428 degrees F. The hotter the oven, the better. Cook for about 10 minutes until the pastry is golden and crisp, and the custard begins to blister.

11. Let the tarts cool down in the tray for a few minutes, then transfer them to a cooling tray.

12. Mix the icing sugar and cinnamon into a bowl, preparing to dust your pastries. You can create a lightning bolt stencil and dust the tart generously.

13. Serve and enjoy warm.

Treacle Fudge

Servings: 18-24 toffees

Prep Time: 25 minutes, 2 hours to cool

Cook Time: 15 minutes

Ingredients:

- 10 ½ oz sugar

- 3 ½ oz butter

- 10 fl oz cream

- ½ tsp vanilla extract

- ¼ tsp salt

- Toppings to decorate (optional)

- Oil for cutting

Instructions:

1. Begin by preparing your tin, greasing it lightly with butter and lining it with baking paper. Then place a pan on medium heat and add in your sugar and butter. Stir it gently until the butter has melted and the mixture has been combined.

2. Using a sugar thermometer, bring the temperature of the mixture up to 250 degrees F, letting it reach the "hard ball" stage. Take the thermometer out and pour in the double cream carefully as the sugar will start to bubble and spit. Let the mixture calm down before stirring.

3. Put in your vanilla and salt next, letting the mixture bubble for 2-3 minutes. Then let the mixture cool in the pan for a couple of minutes; you will notice it thickening.

4. Pour the hot toffee into the tin you prepared and let it cool to room temperature. You can now add any additional toppings you prefer and place the tin in the fridge for 4 hours or overnight.

5. When the fudge has set, you can take the block out of the tin and place it onto the chopping board. Using some oil, grease up your knife and slice the toffee into any preferred shape.

6. Wrap them in wax paper to serve or enjoy as is.

Candy Bark

Servings: 4-6

Prep Time: 10 minutes

Cook Time: 15 minutes

Ingredients:

- Blue candy melts

- Yellow candy melts

- Red candy melts

- Green candy melts

- Candy toppings (optional)

Instructions:

1. Using parchment paper, line a fifteen by eleven half sheet pan and put it aside.

2. Melt the different colour candy melts in the microwave or over a bowl of simmering water.

3. Drop circles of the melted chocolate onto the lined sheet pan and ensure that you are alternating colours, so none of the same colours are next to each other.

4. Taking a knife, smooth the chocolate out and swirl it together.

5. Add the candy toppings of your choice. In this case, we will use jelly slugs.

6. Place it in the fridge for fifteen minutes to chill. Take it out and enjoy it by breaking it or biting it.

Chocolate Frogs

Servings: 16

Prep Time: 10 minutes

Cook Time: 15-20 minutes

Ingredients:

- ¼ cup cold water

- 1 ½ tbsp powdered gelatin

- ½ cup cocoa powder

- ½ cup coconut oil, melted

- ¼ cup granulated sugar

- ¼ cup maple syrup

- ½ tsp vanilla extract

- ¾ cup boiling water

Chocolate Coating

- 2 cups chopped dark chocolate

- 1 tsp cocoa butter

Instructions:

1. Using a stand mixer bowl, mix the cold water with the powdered gelatin and let it bloom for five minutes. While you wait for the gelatin, grease the frog mould with oil lightly, wiping off the excess and setting it aside.

2. Add the cocoa powder, coconut oil, sugar, syrup, and vanilla extract into the same bowl and stir to combine the ingredients until the mixture becomes smooth.

3. Whisk the boiling water into the mix on slow speed and continue to mix until completely smooth.

4. Pour the mixture into the mould and place it into the fridge for three hours until solid. Use your fingers to unmold the frogs by pressing on the edges to release—they should just pop out.

5. Put the frogs on a plate and into the fridge until time to serve. They can also be left without the chocolate coat and served as is.

6. Making the chocolate top coat, melt the chocolate and cocoa butter in a double boiler over hot water. As soon as it becomes smooth, take your frogs from the fridge and quickly dip them in the chocolate one at a time to coat. Tap off the excess chocolate with a fork and place them onto parchment paper. Put your chocolate frogs back into the fridge to allow them to harden.

Fizzing Whizzbees

Servings: 10

Prep Time: 45 minutes

Cook Time: 10-15 minutes

Ingredients:

- ½ cup dark chocolate chips

- 1 packet Pop Rocks candy

Instructions:

1. Using a double boiler or a plastic bowl, melt your chocolate in the microwave in intervals of twenty to thirty seconds, stirring in between to ensure the chocolate doesn't burn. (Previous methods on melting chocolate mentioned in the above recipe can also be used.)

2. Using a bee mould, spoon a thin layer of chocolate into it.

3. Tap the mould on the counter to remove all the air bubbles.

4. Sprinkle a thick layer of pop rocks over the chocolate.

5. Pour another thin layer of chocolate into a mould to cover the pop rocks.

6. Place it into the freezer and let it chill for ten minutes.

7. After 10 minutes, remove them from the freezer and place them into the fridge for another 30 minutes.

8. Now, you can remove the candy from the moulds.

9. Enjoy them as they are or place them in packages with a fun home-made *Fizzy Whizzbees* label on to serve to party guests.

Fudge Flies

Servings: 30-40

Prep Time: 25-30 minutes, 2 hours freezing time

Cook Time: 10-15 minutes

Ingredients:

- 2 cups of white sugar

- ¼ cup dark chocolate melts

- 2 tbsp corn or glucose syrup

- ⅔ cup milk

- 1 tsp vanilla

- 2 tbsp butter

- Pinch of salt

Instructions:

1. In a bowl, melt chocolate in the microwave in intervals of twenty to thirty seconds, stirring in between to ensure the chocolate doesn't burn (previous methods on melting chocolate mentioned in the above recipe can also be used).

2. Pour melted chocolate into a saucepan with the milk, sugar, and corn syrup and bring these ingredients to a boil. Stir them together until they all dissolved.

3. Put in a sugar thermometer and stop stirring, allowing it to boil to the "soft ball" stage.

4. Take the mixture off the stove and add in the butter. Don't stir, instead, let sit until lukewarm.

5. Pour into a mixer and add the vanilla, then beat until creamy.

6. Spoon some fudge into your mould and place them into the freezer to harden quicker.

7. The fudge can be reheated if you are using small moulds by placing them into the microwave in small batches for five to ten seconds. Only reheat what you are going to use.

Exploding Bonbons

Servings: 20

Prep Time: 35 minutes

Cook Time: 1 hour

Ingredients:

- 1 box vanilla cake mix, follow ingredients on box

- ¾ cups vanilla icing

- 1 package each of red, blue, purple, and green Pop Rocks

- 2 cups melted white chocolate

- 3 drops yellow food colouring

- cooking spray

Instructions:

1. Preheat the oven to 350 degrees F and grease a 9x13 pan with cooking spray. Mix the cake mix according to the instructions on the packaging

and bake for about 25 minutes until you can insert a toothpick and it comes out clean. Allow it to cool completely.

2. Crumble the cake into a large bowl, making sure the large pieces are also broken apart. Add in the frosting and stir it until it is completely blended.

3. Roll the mixture into small balls, making wells with your thumb.

4. Place the balls onto a cooling rack and pour the pop rocks into the wells. Seal the pop rocks in with more cake mixture.

5. Freeze cake balls for 30 minutes until they are slightly firm.

6. Now spoon the melted white chocolate over the bonbons, coating them completely.

7. Mix in yellow food colouring to the remaining white chocolate and place it into a piping bag.

8. Decorate each cake ball with lightning bolts and then place them into the freezer for 10 minutes.

Acid Pops

Servings: 10 pops

Prep Time: 8 minutes

Cook Time: 1 minute

Ingredients:

- 10 lollipops

- 8 packages Pop Rocks candy, varying flavours of choice

- ¼ cup Nerds candy (optional)

- ¼ cup honey, warmed

- ¼ cup simple syrup (optional)

Instructions:

1. Heat simple syrup and honey in the microwave for thirty seconds.

2. Unwrap the lollipops, then pour the Nerds and Pop Rocks into separate bowls to allow for easy dipping.

3. For the lollipops with Pop Rocks, dip the end of each lollipop in the warm honey and let excess drip off. Then roll the lollipop in the Pop Rocks quickly and use the palm of your hand to press the Pop Rocks onto the lollipop gently. Arrange them on a plate and let them cool for ten minutes. This is to create a thick layer of Pop Rocks.

4. For the lollipops with a light layer of Pop Rocks, dip the end of each lollipop in the warmed simple syrup and let any excess drip off. Now roll the lollipop in the Pop Rocks quickly and place it on a plate to cool for ten minutes.

5. The lollipops with Nerds can be made by dipping the end of each lollipop in the warmed honey and letting the excess drip off. Then, roll the lollipop in the Nerds and use the palm of your hand to firmly press the Nerds onto the lollipop. Place them on a plate and allow them to cool for ten minutes.

6. Let the candies cool to room temperature before serving them.

Cockroach Clusters

Servings: 5-10

Prep Time: 5 minutes

Cook Time: 1-2 minutes

Ingredients:

- 1 bag dark chocolate chips

- ¼ pound whole pecan halves

- Chocolate candy bar mould

Instructions:

1. Melt the dark chocolate chips in a double boiler until smooth, then spoon about a teaspoon of chocolate into the base of the candy mould.

2. Before the chocolate cools, press two pecan halves into the chocolate, flat side of pecans facing up.

3. Place the moulds in the fridge until they are firm. When they have hardened, pop the chocolate out, and enjoy it, or store them for another day.

Sour Green Worms

Servings: 12

Prep Time: 25 minutes

Cook Time: 7 minutes

Ingredients:

- 1 tsp tapioca pearls (optional, for texture)

- ½ cup tapioca flour

- 1 tbsp rice flour

- 2 tbsp sugar

- 5 tbsp coconut milk

- 2 tbsp lime juice

- 1 drop pandan extract (or natural green colouring)

- A pinch of turmeric

Instructions:

1. Boil water in a small pot and add tapioca pearls to cook for about 5 minutes. Drain the pearls and transfer them to a small bowl, adding one tablespoon of water to keep them from sticking to each other.

2. Then add the tapioca flour, rice flour, and sugar to a mixing bowl and pour in the coconut milk and lime juice. Whisk them together until well combined.

3. Transfer a third of the batter to a small bowl and add a pinch of turmeric, whisk it to combine, then add one drop of pandan extract to the remaining batter and whisk.

4. Bring another pot of water to a boil and place a bamboo steamer basket on top.

5. Grease a six-inch dish that can fit inside your bamboo steamer slightly.

6. Give your mixtures another good stir to ensure the tapioca flour did not set in the bottom. Now pour in a few tablespoons of the green batter into the prepared dish and pour in a tablespoon of the yellow batter. Repeat this process until there is no more batter and you have a third of an inch in thickness. If you are using a small dish, avoid going more than a third of an inch because if it is higher, it might create uneven textures as it will need to steam for longer.

7. Drain your tapioca pearls again and add them to the dish evenly.

8. Move your dish to the bamboo steamer and steam for about 7 minutes until the batter is no longer liquid but still tender. It will firm up a bit more when it cools.

9. Allow it to cool for at least 30 minutes before flipping your dish over onto a lightly oiled surface. Cut the mixture into long thick strips. Keep in mind, the worms will be sticky, so have a little bit of oil on your fingers when working with them to keep them from sticking to you or each other.

Pumpkin Pasties

Servings: 16

Prep Time: 35 minutes, 30 minutes cooling time

Cook Time: 25 minutes

Ingredients:

- 2 ½ cups all-purpose flour

- ½ tsp table salt

- 1 cup salted butter, diced and chilled

- ½ cup very cold ice water

- 1 egg, beaten with 2 tsp water (egg wash)

- coarse sugar for sprinkling

Filling

- 1 cup 100% pure pumpkin puree, canned or homemade

- ¼ cup brown sugar, packed

- 2 tbsp granulated sugar

- ¼ tsp nutmeg

- ½ tsp cinnamon

- ¼ tsp cloves

- ¼ tsp ginger

Glaze

- ½ cup powder sugar

- 1 tbsp whole milk

- ⅛ tsp cinnamon

- ⅛ tsp nutmeg

- ⅛ tsp ginger

- ⅛ tsp cloves

Instructions:

1. Whisk together flour and salt in a large bowl, and using a pastry cutter, cut in the diced cold butter until the mixture resembles coarse crumbs. Small chunks of butter should still be visible. Add in ice water one tablespoon at a time until the mixture holds together when pinched but should not feel sticky. Work the dough sparingly with cold fingers or the pastry cutter, but do not overwork.

2. Form two dough balls, wrap them in plastic, and chill them for at least an hour.

3. Mix all the filling ingredients in a bowl and whisk until well combined.

4. Preheat the oven to 400 degrees F with a rack in the middle position— Line the baking sheets with parchment paper.

5. Roll one of the chilled dough balls to about an eighth of an inch thick on a lightly floured surface. Using a 5-6" diameter bowl rim to cut out circles. Roll the dough again as needed to get as many pieces out as possible.

6. Place two tablespoons of pumpkin filling in the center of each circle. Moisten the edges with water, fold the dough over and then seal the edges tightly. Use a fork to crimp edges and cut slits on top of each one.

Now brush them with egg wash and sprinkle them with coarse sugar. Repeat this process with the remaining dough ball and filling.

7. Bake the pastries on a parchment-lined baking sheet for 25 minutes or until golden brown.

8. Place them on a cooling rack and allow them to cool.

9. Lastly, make the drizzle by combining all the glaze ingredients and whisking them together until smooth. Place it in a Ziploc bag, cut a tiny hole at one corner, and drizzle onto pasties.

Licorice Wands

Servings: 26

Prep Time: 10-15 minutes

Cook Time: 0 minutes

Ingredients:

- 1 cup chocolate chips milk, white, or dark

- 13 licorice sticks of preference

- cookies (crushed)

- sprinkles

- edible glitter

Instructions:

1. Cut the licorice sticks in half.

2. Now, melt the chocolate chips in a microwave-safe bowl by placing them in the microwave, stirring them repeatedly in thirty-second intervals until the chocolate has melted.

3. Transfer the melted chocolate to a tall, skinny glass.

4. Dip the licorice wands about halfway into the melted chocolate and set them down on a parchment-lined plate. Sprinkle with your desired garnish.

5. Move the plate to the fridge and let the chocolate set.

6. Serve the sticks in a tall, skinny glass to display like wands.

CHAPTER III

Did You Say Lunch?

It seems very blatant that most wizards and witches can't think clearly on an empty stomach. This is also true for most non-wizards. Although lunch isn't mentioned as frequently as the snacks on the train or the grand breakfasts and dinners in the great hall, there is a break between classes where the students can go and enjoy their meal of choice, and now you can too!

Herring Fish Cake

Servings: 5-6

Prep Time: 15 minutes

Cook Time: 15-20 minutes

Ingredients:

- 5 oz milk

- 5 oz water

- ½ tsp salt

- ½ tsp pepper

- 1 bay leaf

- ¼ tsp ground nutmeg

- 2 garlic cloves

Herring Fishcakes

- 10 ½ oz whole herring

- 10 ½ oz potato

- 1 tbsp flat-leaf parsley (chopped)

- salt and pepper to taste

- 30 g panko breadcrumbs

- 1 egg

- ½ lemon juice

- 2 tbsp poaching liquid

- 2 oz panko breadcrumbs (coating)

- 4 tbsp oil (for frying)

Instructions:

1. Wash the fresh herring in cold water and pat dry, then remove the head, tail, and fins with your kitchen scissors. Then pull the guts out from the inside.

2. You can cook the herring whole if it is small and remove the bones later on, but for the larger herring, you can fillet the meat from both sides of the skeleton by using a knife.

3. Make your poaching liquid for the fish by placing a saucepan on medium heat and adding in your milk, water, salt, pepper, bay leaf, nutmeg and garlic. Stir and bring the mixture to a boil. Then reduce heat to a low simmer and add in your fish. Cover the fish with a lid and let it cook for ten minutes. Remove the fish from the liquid, setting the liquid aside to use later on for flavouring. Let the fish cool.

4. Peel and chop your potatoes into small rough chunks and boil them in a pot of water for 10-15 minutes until they are nice and soft. Strain the water off and mash the potatoes with a fork, masher, or a ricer.

5. When the fish has cooled, you will be able to remove the remaining bones easily. Then flake the fish using your fork and watching out for large bones that you may have missed.

6. For the fish cakes, put the fish and mashed potatoes into a bowl together, then remove the stems from the parsley and chop it up before adding it into the bowl. Next, add in your salt, pepper, breadcrumbs, eggs, lemon, and two tablespoons of the poaching liquid. Mix through until it is combined evenly.

7. Fishcakes are traditionally circle-shaped, but you can use this chance to shape them however you like. To make lightning bolts, use some plastic wrap and place it onto the surface. Sprinkle some bread crumbs over the wrap to prevent the mixture from sticking to it. Next, add the mixture on top of the breadcrumbs and shape it into one inch thick rectangles. Then use a stencil and cut out your lightning bolts. Scrape together the leftover mixture and repeat the process using all of the mixture.

8. Coat the fishcakes in more of the panko breadcrumbs for an extra crispy coating and set it aside while you heat up your oil on medium to high heat. When the pan is hot, fry the fish cakes for three to five minutes on each side until they turn golden brown.

9. Finish up by baking the fish cakes in the oven at 350 degrees F for 10 minutes. This will make them crispy on the outside and light and fluffy on the inside.

Homemade Bacon

This makes use of the sous vide method, where you place the food in plastic or a glass jar and cook it for much longer than the average cooking time, using very low heat. This will ensure that the food is cooked evenly inside and out, without overcooking the outside. The bacon needs to be cured for a relative amount of days to ensure it retains colour and flavour. It can also be used to preserve the meat for some time.

Servings: Depends on how thick pork cut is - 1 pound serves 4

Prep Time: 45-60 minutes, 10-14 days to cure

Cook Time: 8 hours, 10-15 minutes to fry

Ingredients:

- 4 oz sugar

- 2 oz salt

- 1 tbsp pepper

- 1 tsp celery salt

- 1 tsp coriander

- 1 tsp turmeric

- 1 tsp smoked paprika

- 1 tsp nutmeg

- 2-inch thick pork belly

Instructions:

1. To start with your dry cure bacon rub, add all your ingredients into a bowl and mix together until they are well combined, then set it aside to use later.

2. Wash your pork belly in cold water and remove all the dirt, patting it dry with a kitchen towel and using a sharp knife to score the skin. This will help the cure to permeate the meat. Cover the entire pork belly in your dry bacon rub, doing so generously and massaging it into the meat and skin.

3. Place the pork belly into a Ziploc bag and put it into the fridge for ten to fourteen days, turning the pork belly every two to three days to make sure it cures evenly.

4. When the meat has been cured, it will be firm to the touch, then the dry rub can be rinsed off with cold water and patted dry with a paper towel.

5. For sous vide bacon, place the pork belly into a vacuum bag and seal it. Cook it in your sous vide at 145 degrees F for 8 hours. Soon as it is cooked, you can let it cool quickly by placing it into an ice bath.

6. Take the pork out from the vacuum bag and pat it dry again, then slice the bacon as thick or as thin as you would prefer it.

7. Warm a pan on medium heat and fry the bacon. Depending on how thick you sliced the bacon, it varies in cooking time. Fry until crispy and golden brown, then flip and repeat on the other side. Drain off the extra oil with a kitchen towel and then serve and enjoy.

Hundred Layer Chicken & Ham Sandwich

Servings: 10-12

Prep Time: 20-30 minutes

Cook Time: 5-10 minutes

Ingredients:

- 2 red onions

- 1 tbsp oil

- pinch salt

- pepper (to taste)

- 2 tbsp brown sugar

- 1/2 tbsp balsamic vinegar

- 5 tbsp mayonnaise

- 1/2 tbsp wholegrain mustard

- 2 oz margarine/butter

- 1 small lettuce

- 6 tomatoes

- 20-30 slices of chicken

- 20-30 slices of ham

- skewers (for support)

- white bread

Instructions:

1. Cut your onions in half and slice them into thin rings. Heat a pan with oil in it and add the onions, stirring it for 5 minutes until they start turning golden. Use salt and pepper to season and add in the balsamic vinegar and sugar, stirring for 2-3 minutes until the sauce thickens. Move from the pan into a bowl and let it cool.

2. Then add the mayonnaise and mustard into a bowl and mix them together until combined.

3. Wash and rinse your tomatoes and lettuce, and then slice them both into thin rounds and shreds.

4. Now lay out bread and begin to stack the layers, starting with bread and butter and alternating each layer with filling and additional bread slices, using the skewers to keep the layers from collapsing, until you reach your goal. Don't rush the process. Take your time and steady the sandwich as you go.

5. Enjoy!

Cursed Chicken Nuggets

Servings: 25 -28

Prep Time: 15 minutes

Cook Time: 15 minutes

Ingredients:

- 1 pound ground chicken

- 1 teaspoon garlic powder

- 1 teaspoon onion powder

- 2 cups bread crumbs

Instructions:

1. Preheat the oven to 350 degrees F.

2. Line a baking tray with parchment paper.

3. Spread breadcrumbs on a plate to dip in the shaped chicken nuggets.

4. Add the ground chicken into a large bowl.

5. Add your seasonings and stir to combine (using your hands to mash it together is easier). The seasoning can also be switched up or kept the same for taste.

6. To create the a shape, roll out a log shape from the mixture and coat it in breadcrumbs. Lay the covered log on some parchment paper and shape it into the lightning scar. Shaping is easier once the mixture has been coated in breadcrumbs.

7. To make the glasses, repeat the same steps as above, but when shaping the glasses, make two circles and connect them in the center with a small nose-bridge and put it all together on the parchment paper.

8. Repeat until you have used all the ground chicken.

9. Bake for 20 minutes at 350 degrees F. Thinner parts may take less time to cook. Shapes may take a bit longer to cook.

Spiced Plum Cake

Servings: 10-12

Prep Time: 20 minutes

Cook Time: 70 minutes

Ingredients:

- 6 oz butter

- 6 oz golden caster sugar

- 3 eggs

- 6 oz self-raising flour

- 1 tsp vanilla extract

- ¼ tsp mixed spice

- ¼ tsp cinnamon

- 3 plums (ripe)

- 2 tbsp self-raising flour

- 3 ½ oz plain flour

- 2 oz butter

- 2 oz golden caster sugar

- ½ tsp ground ginger

- 1 plum

- 2 tbsp golden syrup

Instructions:

1. Start by making the spice plum cake batter by creaming together the butter and sugar until it becomes light and fluffy.

2. Then crack the eggs into a jug and whisk them together until they are even. Now pour them into the butter and sugar while mixing it on a slow speed. Add a tablespoon of flour to the mixture if it seems to be splitting or curdling.

3. Add in the flour, vanilla, mixed spice, and cinnamon and keep whisking the mixture on a low speed until it is combined. Don't overmix, as it will leave you with a dense sponge cake.

4. Cut the plums in half, remove the seeds and then chop them into small chunks. Throw the chunks into the leftover flour to keep them from sinking and then fold them into the batter.

5. Take a 7-inch baking tin, grease and line before pouring in the cake batter and use a spatula to level it off.

6. Place flour and butter into the bowl and, using your fingertips, work it to form chunky breadcrumbs. Add in your sugar and ginger, and then mix to combine well. Sprinkle this over the cake generously.

7. Slice and remove the seeds from the leftover plums and cut them into thin strips. Place the strips on the crumble of the cake in the shape or initial that you desire.

8. Using golden syrup, glaze the fruit and then bake the plum in the oven at 350 degrees F for 30-40 minutes or until the crumble becomes golden.

9. Glaze the fruit again when you remove the cake from the oven and allow it cool for 10 minutes before taking it out of the pan. This can be served hot or cold.

CHAPTER IV

Dinner, A History

Great Britain consists of a large and diverse history and a rich culture. This could be because there are three very different countries that are connected (England, Wales and Scotland) and why the traditions connected to food also vary. Looking at the history of Britain, one can see how it played a noteworthy part in the development of the culture and food it has today. The country has also been known as a trading nation, and with the variety of goods they came in contact with, it is no surprise that the food became more colourful and diverse. The meals that are enjoyed can tell you a lot about the culture and people of a country, food being strongly connected by their dishes. This is also true for the way they gather around the food and the events they serve certain dishes at. Wizardry is not any different, and it is clear that they are rooted in the traditions of the Scottish, Irish and English culture.

When Harry first arrived at Hogwarts, he received a lavish feast during the Sorting Ceremony. This, however, is not the only time students indulge in large, traditional meals. Harry and his friends enjoy multiple traditional meals during their time at Hogwarts, ranging from kippers to shepherds pie and many more! The world of some of these foods are a bit intimidating to the people looking in on the strange meals, but once you give the delicacies a try, you might be surprised at what you end up finding enjoyable and delicious!

Steak and Kidney Pie

Servings: 6

Prep Time: 40 minutes

Cook Time: 2 hours 40 minutes

Ingredients:

- 1.7 oz unsalted butter

- 2 tbsp olive oil

- 2 onions, chopped

- 9 oz Swiss brown mushrooms

- 28 oz beef chuck steak, cut into ⅔ of an inch cubes

- 7 oz veal kidneys or lamb kidneys rimmed, cut into ⅔-inch cubes

- 2 tbsp plain flour, seasoned

- 2 garlic cloves, chopped

- 11 fl oz bottle stout (such as Guinness)

- 1 ½ cups (12.6 fl oz) beef stock

- 2 bay leaves

- 2 thyme sprigs, leaves picked, plus extra for garnish

- 1 tbsp tomato paste

- 2 tbsp HP sauce (optional)

- 2 tbsp chopped flat-leaf parsley

- 13 oz block frozen puff pastry, thawed

- 1 egg, beaten

Instructions:

1. In an ovenproof casserole dish, melt the butter and one tablespoon of oil over medium heat. Add in the onions and cook them while stirring for two to three minutes. Then add the mushrooms and cook the mixture for another two minutes. Remove from the heat and set the onion mixture aside.

2. Add a tablespoon of oil to a pan and toss the kidneys in some flour. Cook the kidneys in the pan over medium heat, turning them as they cook, for 2-3 minutes to seal both sides. Set aside.

3. Now add the beef and cover it with the remaining flour, then, in two parts, cook the beef for 4-5 minutes until it is brown on both sides. Then add in the kidney and onion to the pan again, add in stout and bring to a boil. Reduce the heat and let simmer for 8-10 minutes until reduced by half.

4. Next, add in stock, herbs, tomato paste and some salt and pepper, bringing it to a boil and again reducing the heat to low. Cover it partially and leave it to simmer for an hour and a half. Stir the mixture occasionally until the meat is soft.

5. Take the meat and the vegetables out with a slotted spoon and throw away the leaves, then leave the sauce over medium heat for five to six minutes to simmer until it is reduced by a cup and a half. Next, stir in HP sauce and parsley, returning the meat and vegetables to the pan and leaving it cool.

6. Preheat the oven to 392 degrees F.

7. Roll out your pastry on a floured workspace until it is five millimetres thick. Cut a half an inch strip of pastry that will fit the border of a 33.8 fl oz pie dish, using the pie dish as a template to cut the pastry lids half an inch larger than the dish.

8. Divide the pie mixture among the dishes and press the pastry strips around the pie dish rims, brushing it with water. Place the pastry lids on top of the dish and trim off the excess pastry. Seal the edges with a fork and brush it with egg wash. Top the pastry with thyme sprigs, then bake it for twenty-five minutes or until the pastry is puffed and golden.

Bouillabaisse

Servings: 4

Prep Time: 30 minutes

Cook Time: 2 hours

Ingredients:

- 1 baguette, sliced into ½-inch pieces

- 3 large tomatoes peeled, seeds out and coarsely chopped

- ½ cup sweet onion, chopped

- 2 leeks whites only, finely julienned

- 4 cloves garlic, minced

- 1 pound potatoes cut into bite-sized chunks

- 4 medium carrots, sliced diagonally into ½-inch pieces

- 1/2 cup olive oil

- 2 tbsp tomato paste

- 2 bay leaves

- 1 tbsp fennel, finely chopped

- 1 tbsp lemon zest

- ½ tsp saffron threads, crumbled

- 3 tbsp fresh parsley, chopped

- 1 ½ tbsp sea salt

- 1 tsp fresh ground black pepper

- 4 cups of fish stock

- 2 pounds of white fish fillets, bones removed and cut into 2-inch pieces

- ½ pound small hard-shelled clams such as Little Neck, scrubbed

- ½ pound mussels, scrubbed and any beards removed

- ½ pound prawns in shells

- ½ pound lobster meat, cut into 1-inch pieces

Rouille

- 3 tbsp water

- ¾ cup coarse fresh bread crumbs from a baguette crust removed

- 3 garlic cloves

- ½ teaspoon sea salt

- ½ teaspoon cayenne

- 3 tbsp extra virgin olive oil

Instructions:

1. Preheat the oven to 250 degrees F. Prepare the baguette croutons by removing the crusts, brushing them lightly with olive oil and arranging them on a baking sheet. Bake for 30 minutes, then rub one side with fresh garlic. Set it aside until the stew is ready.

2. Cook the tomatoes, onion, leeks and garlic in oil over medium heat, using a large Dutch oven, occasionally stirring, until the onion is soft and transparent for about 5-7 minutes.

3. Peel the potatoes and cut them into bite-sized cubes. Stir the potatoes and carrots into the tomato mix and add the tomato paste, fennel, bay leaf, saffron, parsley, sea salt, and pepper.

4. Add the fish stock and bring to a boil. Then lower the heat, cover, and simmer it until the potatoes are almost tender for 8-10 minutes.

5. Add any thicker pieces of fish, scallops and clams and simmer it while covered for two minutes. Stir in the mussels, shrimp, lobster, and remaining fish, then simmer the covered mixture for 5 minutes. The mussels should now have opened.

6. Stir approximately three tablespoons of broth from the stew into the roux until it's smooth and well blended.

7. Then arrange a layer of croutons in wide, shallow bowls. Using a slotted spoon, transfer the seafood onto the croutons, then ladle some hot broth and vegetables around the edges of the croutons. Also, add a dab of rouille on top and serve it immediately.

8. Next, using a small mixing bowl, pour the water over the bread crumbs. Mash garlic with the flat edge of a knife and mix it into a paste with sea salt and cayenne. Add it to the moistened bread crumbs with the Dijon mustard, mixing all of it into a garlic paste.

9. Add the oil in a thin stream slowly, mixing it vigorously until it is well blended.

10. Add a clump of the Rouille on top of the bouillabaisse just before serving it, and serve the rest on the side along with some crusty French bread.

Roast Chicken

Servings: 5

Prep Time: 15 minutes

Cook Time: 1 hour 30 minutes

Ingredients:

- 1 whole chicken (3 ½ to 4 pounds)

- 2 large cloves of garlic

- 1 large yellow onion, cut into wedges

- 1 lemon, cut in half

- 4 tbsp unsalted butter, softened

- 1 tbsp Italian parsley, chopped

- 1 tbsp fresh thyme, chopped

- 2 bay leaves

- sea salt & ground black pepper

Instructions:

1. Preheat the oven to 400 degrees F.

2. Stuff the onion wedges, lemon halves, bay leaves, and garlic into the chicken cavity.

3. Mix the softened butter with parsley, thyme, salt and pepper, and rub it all over the chicken.

4. Place it in a roasting pan and roast it for approximately 1 hour and 15 minutes to an hour and a half, working it out about 15 minutes per pound, or until the juices run clear when you pierce the thickest part with a skewer.

5. Remove the roast from the oven and set it aside to rest for 10 minutes before serving it with crispy roast potatoes and gravy.

Roast Beef

Servings: 6

Prep Time: 2 hours 10 minutes

Cook Time: 1 hour

Ingredients:

- 3 lbs rump roast (boneless)

- 3 tsp salt

- 1 tbsp olive oil

- 3 cloves garlic (sliced in half or thirds)

- 1 tsp pepper

Instructions:

1. Thaw the roast in the fridge the night before you want to cook.

2. Remove the roast from the refrigerator, letting it come to room temperature for about one hour before cooking.

3. Rub two teaspoons of salt on the roast while it sits covered.

4. Preheat the oven to 375 degrees F. Then make small slits in the roast and put in sliced pieces of garlic in each of the slits.

5. Rub the meat with olive oil and sprinkle it with salt and pepper to taste.

6. Place the roast directly on the middle oven rack with a pan underneath to catch the dripping, and bake it for thirty minutes. Afterward, lower the temperature down to 225 degrees F.

7. Bake it for another hour and a half to two and a half hours, until the internal temperature of the roast reaches 135 degrees F.

8. Remove the roast from the oven and place it on a jelly roll pan. Next, make a tent out of tin foil to cover the roast and let it rest for 20-30 minutes.

9. Cut the roast into thin slices and serve it.

Shepherd's Pie

Servings: 4

Prep Time: 15 minutes

Cook Time: 50 minutes

Ingredients:

- 1 red onion

- 2 small carrots

- 1 stick celery

- 1 tbsp oil

- 2-3 garlic cloves

- 14 oz diced lamb

- salt and pepper

- 3.4 fl oz red wine

- 15.8 oz tomato passata

- 1 tbsp tomato puree

- 1 lamb (or beef) stock cube

- 1 tsp mixed herbs

- ½ tsp nutmeg

- ½ tsp cinnamon

- a few dashes of Worcestershire sauce

- 4 medium-large white potatoes

- 2 medium sweet potatoes

- 1.7-3.5 oz mature cheddar

- 1.7 oz butter

- 1.6 fl oz milk

- salt and pepper

- parsley to garnish

Instructions:

1. Make the lamb ragu base by chopping up the onion, celery, and carrots finely. Add oil into a pan, placing it on medium heat before stirring in vegetables. Keep it moving around for 3-5 minutes until they have started to turn translucent.

2. Peel and crush garlic before adding it to the pan and cooking it for another minute. Take off the vegetables and put them aside in a bowl.

3. Sear the lamb by adding it into the pan, seasoning the meat with salt and pepper and then turning it after about 20-30 seconds on each side, giving it time to go brown, but not cooking it through. Take the lamb off of the pan and set it aside.

4. Deglaze the pan using the red wine and let it bubble for about 30 seconds as this helps remove the caramelization from the bottom of the pan to increase the flavour. The alcohol also burns away, so it is child friendly.

5. Pour tomato passata and puree into the pan along with the vegetables, lamb and the assorted seasonings: salt, pepper, mixed herbs, nutmeg, cinnamon, stock cube and Worchester sauce. Place a lid on the top, turn the heat down to the lowest setting and leave it to simmer for one to two hours. The lamb will also tenderize during this step.

6. While the lamb is bubbling away, you can get the mashed potatoes ready by peeling and washing your potatoes. Leave them in cold water when they have been peeled to keep them from turning brown.

7. Boil the white and sweet potatoes in separate pots of boiling water, seasoned with salt, for ten to fifteen minutes. Check by testing if easily pierced with a fork.

8. When it's ready, strain off the water using a colander and mash the potatoes in a bowl using a masher, ricer or fork. Flavour your potatoes with salt, pepper, butter, milk and cheese, mixing it thoroughly until everything has melted and combined. Then flavour the sweet potatoes with salt, pepper, and butter.

9. To decorate, place the mashed potatoes into a piping bag with a star nozzle.

10. Half an hour before the lamb is ready, take the lid off to encourage the fluid to vaporize and give you a thicker, richer sauce. When it is ready, pour it into the bottom of your roasting dish and smooth off with a spatula.

11. Pipe the mashed potato on top of the foundation, starting creating the lightning bolt out of sweet potato and then continuing your way around the outside with the white potato mash. To get a thicker layer of mash, you can then go over the top again with each.

12. When you're happy with the pattern, bake the shepherd's pie in the oven at 350 degrees F for 25-30 minutes until the potatoes have just started to turn a golden brown. Sprinkle some parsley over the top just before you serve.

French Onion Soup

Servings: 6

Prep Time: 10 minutes

Cook Time: 1 hour 10 minutes

Ingredients:

- 17.6 oz onions

- 1.7 oz butter

- 1 tbsp olive oil

- 4 garlic cloves

- salt and pepper

- 3 sprigs rosemary

- 3 sprigs thyme

- 1 bay leaf

- 2.5 fl oz white wine

- 16.9 fl oz strong beef stock

- 6 slices of bread

- 1 tbsp butter

- 1 garlic clove

- 3.5 oz gruyere cheese, grated

- 1 tsp fresh or dried parsley

Instructions:

1. Make the base by peeling and chopping the onions. Remove the skins, slice them in half and then slice them thinly. Use a food processor with a slicing attachment to chop the onions if you aren't used to doing so in large amounts.

2. Place a pan on medium to low heat and then add in your butter and olive oil, swirling it until the butter has melted. Next, add in the onions and allow them to fry for about 10 minutes until they turn soft and translucent. If the onions begin to catch fire, add olive oil to keep them from burning.

3. Peel the cloves of garlic, crush them with a garlic press and then add it to the onions. Season the base with salt, pepper, finely chopped rosemary and thyme and then add to the base. Stir thoroughly and let it continue cooking on low heat for 15-20 minutes.

4. Once the onions are dark and golden, deglaze the pan by pouring in the white wine. Stir through as it bubbles away, then add in the beef stock and bay leaf and stir it well. Give the soup a taste test, adding in any extra salt and pepper to taste and then place a lid on top, allowing the soup to simmer for 20 minutes.

5. For the garlic cheese croutons, prepare slices of bread by cutting them small or use baguette slices. Melt the butter in a pan and crush your garlic before adding. Allow it to fry for a minute.

6. Add the bread and toast for 1-2 minutes on each side until it turns golden.

7. Transfer the soup into ramekins, leaving an inch gap from the top. Place the croutons over the ramekin and sprinkle a generous amount of the cheese over the top. Finish it with some parsley before placing it under the grill for 3-5 minutes until the cheese has melted into the soup. Serve warm.

Pumpkin Soup

Servings: 8

Prep Time: 15 minutes

Cook Time: 1 hour

Ingredients:

- 1 red onion
- 3 celery sticks
- 3 carrots
- 1 tbsp butter
- 1 medium pumpkin
- 1 small butternut squash
- 1 red pepper
- salt and pepper
- 1 tsp cumin
- 1 tsp paprika
- 1 tsp coriander
- 1 tsp turmeric
- 1 tsp mixed herbs
- 1 vegetable stock cube
- 8 cups of hot water

- 1 tsp olive oil

- ¼ tsp ground ginger

- 1 tbsp butter

- Sprig of fresh coriander

Instructions:

1. Prepare vegetable base (also known as a mirepoix) by chopping the onion, carrots, and celery into small chunks. Melt butter in the pan and add in the vegetables, stirring it for 3-5 minutes until sweated and glossy. Season it with salt and pepper.

2. Ready the rest of the vegetables by peeling the pumpkin and butternut squash and use a serrated knife to cut it into chunks. Keep the seeds to one side for a quick and healthy topping. Remove the seeds from the pepper and chop them into chunks.

3. Add the vegetables into a large pan and stir thoroughly. If the pan seems full, split the content into two. Season the vegetables with mixed herbs, ground coriander, cumin, paprika, and turmeric. Mix well until evenly seasoned, and add in your stock cube with hot water. Cover and leave it to simmer for 30 minutes.

4. While the soup is simmering, prepare your pumpkin seeds as a healthy crouton alternative. Drizzle the oil into a pan, and then add in your pumpkin seeds before seasoning it with salt, pepper, and ginger. Combine it until evenly coated, and then roast it in the oven at 350 degrees F for 15-20 minutes until they turn golden.

5. As soon as the vegetables are soft and cooked through, move them into a bowl and use a hand blender to get a smooth soup. Add more vegetable stock if the soup is too thick.

6. Add in a knob of butter and stir it through until it melted to get a smooth and velvety finish. Season it with any additional salt and pepper

and pour it into your bowls. Top it off with a garnish of your roast pumpkin seeds, cream, and coriander just before serving.

Roast Pork Wellington

Servings: 6

Prep Time: 45 minutes

Cook Time: 1 hour

Ingredients:

- 1 cooking apple

- 0.5 oz butter

- 0.5 oz sugar

- salt and pepper

- 2.9 oz stuffing mix

- 1 tbsp butter

- 6.7 fl oz boiling water

- 1 pork tenderloin

- salt and pepper

- Rosemary and thyme

- 10.5 oz puff pastry

- 1 egg

- 2 tbsp milk

Instructions:

1. To make the applesauce, start by chopping the apple into chunks, but keep from cutting them too small as they will cook away.

2. Place the apples, sugar, and butter into a pan on medium heat and cook for five to ten minutes until the apples have softened. Season them with salt and pepper and continue stirring them until some of the apples have broken down, but still leaving you with some texture. Set aside the mixture to cool.

3. To make the stuffing, pour your mix into a bowl with the butter and pour over the boiling water. Mix it together until well combined and let stand for 5 minutes.

4. Season your pork tenderloin with salt, pepper, rosemary and thyme. Heat up your frying pan on medium to high heat and add a little bit of oil before searing the outside of the pork until golden brown - this should not take more than 60 seconds on each side.

5. Double line your counter with plastic wrap and spread it over a thin, even layer of stuffing, the same length as your pork tenderloin. Spread the apple sauce over the top of this, and then place the pork along the edge closest to you.

6. Using the plastic wrap to help you, roll the stuffing and apple sauce over the pork and seal it. Roll the sausage back and forth to form an even and uniform shape. Then place it in the fridge to chill for thirty minutes.

7. Roll the puff pastry out on a lightly floured surface. Remove the pork from the plastic wrap and place it at one end of the puff pastry. Beat the egg and milk together to create the egg wash and brush some of this on the edge of the pastry. Then roll the pork, so it is completely sealed with pastry. Using some more egg wash, stick the edges down.

8. Use any leftover pastry to cut out the lightning bolt and star shapes for decorations, then use the egg wash to help stick these down. Give the entire wellington a final egg wash and then bake in the oven at 350 degrees F for 40 minutes.

9. When the wellington is golden brown, let it rest for five to ten minutes before moving it to a serving dish and slicing it. Serve it immediately.

Haggis

This Scottish dish is a savoury pudding of sorts and consists of sheep's pluck, minced with onion, oatmeal, suet, spices, and salt, mixed with stock. Traditionally, the casing would be an animal stomach, but artificial casings are more common nowadays.

Servings: 4

Prep Time: 35 minutes

Cook Time: 4 hours 15 minutes

Ingredients:

- 2-3 sprigs of rosemary

- 2-3 sprigs of thyme

- 2 bay leaves

- 4 garlic cloves

- 1 vegetable stock cube

- 14.1 oz diced lamb

- 7 oz liver

- 1 onion

- 5.2 oz oatmeal

- 2.6 oz suet

- ½ tsp ground nutmeg

- ½ tsp ground coriander

- sausage skins

- 4 white potatoes

- 1 large suede

- salt and pepper

- 1.7 oz butter

- 1.6 oz milk

- ½ tsp wholegrain mustard

- ¼ tsp ground nutmeg

- Salt and pepper

Instructions:

1. To make the meat for the haggis, make a vegetable broth by adding about 4 ¼ cups of water into a pan and bring it to a boil. Season it with salt and pepper, rosemary, thyme and bay leaves. Next, peel the garlic cloves and add them in along with the vegetable stock cube, stirring it until it dissolved.

2. Add in the diced lamb and liver before turning the heat down to a simmer. Scoop off any scum that forms on the top, placing a lid on top and letting it cook for 2 hours until the meat has tenderized.

3. As soon as it's cooked, remove the meat from the broth and leave it to cool. Keep the broth to use in the haggis mixture. Bring back to a boil and boil rapidly until around 1 cup of a rich sauce is left.

4. When the meat is cool enough to handle, you can finely chop the lamb and liver until it looks like a crumbly texture.

5. To create the haggis filling, grate the onion, crush the garlic cloves that were infusing the broth, and finely chop some rosemary and thyme.

6. Add the haggis meat, onion, garlic, oatmeal, suet, and seasonings: salt, pepper, rosemary, thyme, nutmeg and coriander. Mix thoroughly until combined evenly.

7. Pour the reduced stock into the haggis mixture and stir through. If it looks too watery, don't worry, as the oatmeal and suet will absorb the moisture.

8. Move the haggis filling into a piping bag (or a sausage machine), placing the sausage skins on the end and tying a knot at the end. Squeeze out the mixture to fill the sausage skins about half full, being careful not to overfill them as they will burst when being cooked.

9. Create long sausages, around 7.8 inches in length, tying the sausage skins at the end and cutting it. Make a new knot for the next sausage and repeat the process until all the mixture is used up.

10. Lightly grease a baking tray and then place your haggis sausages in it, shaping them into lightning bolts. You can use skewers to keep them in place. Roast the haggis in the oven at 350 degrees F for 15-20 minutes until they turn nice and golden.

11. For the neeps and tatties, peel your potatoes and suede. Chop them into rough small pots and then boil them for 10-15 minutes in different pans until they turn nice and soft.

12. Strain the vegetables and then season the potatoes with salt, pepper, milk, butter and wholegrain mustard before mashing them. It's the same process for the suede but season it with salt, pepper, butter, and nutmeg.

13. Lastly, plate up the dish and for an added touch, pipe the neeps and tatties into lightning bolts next to the haggis and enjoy.

CHAPTER V

Treat Yourself

Comfort food is one of the most common ways we, as non-magic folk, use in times of darkness. They can cure whatever causes the discomfort by lifting morale and helping us forget whatever it is that is plaguing us. Treats, however, have a different effect for wizards, as it may have some magical spell that is placed onto it. This is done to lift the spirits of young wizards and to entertain them. Think of the chocolate covered frogs that have a charm placed on them to behave like real frogs, if only for one hop.

Toffee Apples

Creating the perfect quidditch toffee apples is no easy feat! It does take a little bit of trial-and-error to complete the details. It might help to practice the designs before adding them to your apples.

Servings: 4

Prep Time: 35 minutes

Cook Time: 30 minutes

Ingredients:

• Fresh apples (1 large cooking apple for the Quaffle, 2 medium-sized to Bludgers, 1 mini apples for the Snitch)

• 14 oz granulated sugar

• 3.5 oz liquid glucose or corn syrup

• 4.2 fl oz water

• Yellow, red, and black food colouring

• Silver and gold luster dust

• Mixing alcohol or vodka

• 1.7 oz white candy melts

Instructions:

1. Prepare apples by cleaning them thoroughly in cold water and patting them dry completely using a paper towel. Moisture will keep the sugar coating from setting.

2. Take off stems and use a sharp skewer to pierce the middle of the apples, being careful not to go all the way through.

3. Next, place a saucepan on medium to high heat and add in your sugar, glucose, and water. Do not stir, if you need to assist the sugar with dissolving, gently swirl the pan. Add in a sugar thermometer and bring the mixture to a boil. Keep heating it until it reaches the 'soft crack' stage at 280 degrees F.

4. Turn the heat off and swirl in your lightest colour first, this being yellow for the golden Snitch. When you have an even colour, dip the mini apple in and get an even coating, twisting it in your hand until it stops dripping. Place on a silicone mat and leave it to set.

5. Next, add red colouring to the sugar for the Quaffle and dip your largest apple in, twirl it to get an even coat and set it down. Redo this step for the bludgers, adding in black and red food colouring, twirl and place it aside to set.

6. To decorate the bludgers, make a silver paint with luster dust and mixing alcohol and make a swirl around the ball. Leave it to dry for a few minutes.

7. For the Quaffle candy apple decor, mix gold paint with gold dusting and mixing alcohol to paint on the Hogwarts crest. Then use black food colouring and mixing alcohol to create contour circles.

8. For the Golden Snitch toffee apple design, melt your white candy melts and place them into a piping bag. Draw your wings on some wax paper and pipe over them, filling in the centers. Leave it to set while you make your silver paint and colour the chocolate wings silver. Use edible gold glitter spray to paint the Snitch. When it's dry, use a little more melted chocolate to the sides of the apple.

Nearly Headless Headstone Cake

Sculpting a headstone for a cake can be a bit of a challenge, but with some practice, it can be done without breaking a sweat! For some of the finer details, if you are afraid of going free-handed, stencils might be useful. You could also print out a design on some edible paper to simplify the decorations.

Servings: 24

Prep Time: 25 minutes, 30-45 minutes decorating

Cook Time: 35 minutes

Ingredients:

• 24 oz butter

- 24 oz golden caster sugar

- 12 eggs

- 24 oz self-raising flour

- 4 tbsp cocoa powder

- 3.3 fl oz boiling water

- 1 tsp ground mixed spice

- 1 tbsp + 1 tsp vanilla extract

- 10.5 oz butter

- 21 oz icing sugar

- 2 tbsp milk

- black food colouring

- 1 egg white

- 8.8 oz icing sugar

- ¼ tsp lemon juice

- 26.5 oz white fondant icing

- 5 marshmallows

Instructions:

1. Start by creaming the butter and sugar together for two to three minutes until it is light and fluffy. Crack the eggs into a jug and whisk them lightly before adding them into the butter and sugar, doing so a little at a time, whisking as you go. If the mixture starts to curdle, add a spoonful of flour to bind it again.

2. When the eggs are combined with the mixture, scrape down the sides and add in the flour, mixed spice, and a tablespoon of vanilla. Make a paste by stirring together the cocoa powder and hot water before adding it to the cake mix.

3. Beat everything together until they are combined, being careful not to over-mix the cake batter. Then grease and line an 11-inch square baking tin and pour in the cake mixture. Level it off with a spatula and bake it in the oven at 350 degrees F for 35-40 minutes until a skewer comes out clean.

4. While the cake is cooling, make the buttercream icing by whisking the butter for 10-20 minutes. Once smooth, add the icing sugar in thirds, whisking slowly in between intervals. Add in the milk and teaspoon of vanilla and whisk for another 2-3 minutes until light and fluffy. Use the black food colouring to dye the icing grey for the tombstone.

5. Next, use a serrated knife to level the sponge and then cut it into even rectangles. Placing the first down onto a board, add an even layer of buttercream on top and sandwich the next layer on top. Repeat until all the cake layers are stacked. Chill the cake in the fridge for an hour.

6. Once the cake is chilled, place the cake on its side and use a stencil to cut out the tombstone cake. You can also secure it with cake dowels before standing the cake up. Crumb coat the outside with a thin layer of buttercream and return the cake to the fridge for another hour.

7. Dye the fondant grey with some more black food colouring, leaving the dye slightly marbled for an added texture effect, and then roll it out to quarter-inch thick.

8. Ice the back of the tombstone, smoothing it into place before trimming it down. Lay the cake down and then ice the front of the cake with the remaining fondant. Use the trimmings to create your additional fondant decorations - a trim around the outside of the tombstone, 'RIP' letterings and some decorative leaves.

9. For the royal icing, whisk the egg white until foamy and then add in the icing sugar, whisking it until it's smooth. Add in the lemon juice and

food colouring and continue to whisk. Transfer it into a piping bag with a writing tip before piping your message onto the front of the tombstone.

10. Create soil with the leftover cake trimmings by crumbling them with your hands and spreading them over your cake board. You can then stand the cake up at the top of the 'grave.'

11. Add the final decoration for a spooky effect by melting the marshmallows in the microwave for 10-20 seconds. Allow it to cool for 20 seconds, and dip your fingers into the marshmallows, stretching it to form cobwebs. Place as few or as many as you like over the top of the cake.

Cartoon Cheesecake

Servings: 8-12

Prep Time: 30-45 minutes, 3-4 hours chill time or overnight

Cook Time: 0 minutes

Ingredients:

Filling

- 4 gelatin sheets

- 1.5 fl oz water

- 5.2 oz white chocolate

- 1.7 oz butter

- 1.7 oz sugar

- 21 oz cream cheese

- 6.7 fl oz double cream

- yellow food colouring

Cookie Base

- 3.5 oz ginger cookies

- 1.7 oz butter (melted)

- green food colouring

- gummy worms

Instructions:

1. To make the cheesecake filling, start by blooming the gelatin, placing the sheets into a bowl of cold water and leaving it aside for 5 minutes until soft.

2. Place a glass bowl over simmering water and add in your chocolate, stirring it until it's completely melted and smooth. Place this aside to cool.

3. Return the bowl to the pan of water and add in the butter and sugar. Mix it thoroughly until the sugar has completely dissolved, and then add in the bloomed gelatin and water. Stir it through until the gelatin has dissolved as well.

4. Add the cream cheese into a mixer and whisk it until it is smooth while pouring in the cream a little at a time. Add in the chocolate and gelatin mixture and keep on whisking as the mixture thickens up. You can now add in the yellow food colouring to give it a true cartoon cheese colour.

5. For the base (which is going to be the mould in the cheesecake), add the ginger cookies into a food processor and blend them until they form fine crumbs. Transfer the crumbs into a bowl and whisk in some green food colouring into your melted butter. Then pour into the cookies, stirring through until you have your green ''mould crumbs.

6. To put the cheesecake together, line the base of a 7-inch loose bottom tin and lightly grease the sides. Add in some of the cheesecake mixture evenly. Sprinkle over some of the green mould and then cover it with more of the cheesecake filling to hide the mould inside. Repeat the process until all the mixture has been used, finishing with a layer of the cheesecake filling.

7. Use an offset spatula to level off the top and then place the cheesecake in the fridge to set for 3-4 hours. It is recommended to leave it overnight for the best results. When it has set, use a blowtorch to heat up the sides lightly and ease it out of the baking tin and onto a serving dish.

8. Warm a spoon, melon baller or an ice cream scoop in some hot water and then scoop out sporadic circles of the cheesecake to create your cartoon cheese holes.

9. Use some of the leftover cookies to place into the holes and around the board before adding the gummy worms to make it look like they are crawling in and out of the cake.

10. Place the cake back into the fridge until ready to serve. You can keep it in the fridge to enjoy for up to 3 days.

Grape Tart

Servings: 6-8

Prep Time: 20-30 minutes

Cook Time: 20-25 minutes

Ingredients:

Shortcrust Pastry

- 5.2 oz plain flour

- pinch of salt

- 2.6 oz butter

- 1.7 oz icing sugar

- 1 egg yolk

- 1-2 tbsp cold water

Filling

- 1 punnet of grapes (approx. 17.6 oz)

- 2 tbsp maple syrup

- ¼ tsp cinnamon

- 1.7 oz soft brown sugar

Cream

- 10 fl oz milk

- 2 tbsp golden caster sugar

- 1 tbsp cornflour

- 2 egg yolks

- 1 egg

- 1 tsp vanilla extract

- 5 fl oz double cream

Instructions:

1. Make the shortcrust pastry by placing the flour into a bowl with the salt and stir it together. Add in the room temperature butter and work it

together with your fingers until it forms breadcrumbs. Stir through the icing sugar and make a well in the middle.

2. Next, add the egg yolk and water into the middle and bind it together using a knife. Use your hands to form a smooth ball of dough and wrap it in plastic wrap before placing it in the fridge to chill for 15 minutes.

3. Lightly flour your workstation and roll the pastry out to a quarter of an inch thick. Lift the pastry up using a rolling pin and transfer it into your tart tin, working it into the sides and bottom. Then prick the bottom with a fork to prevent it from rising. Cover the pastry with parchment paper and fill it with baking beans—Bake at 350 degrees F for 10 minutes.

4. Take out the baking beans and parchment paper, trim down the sides to make it neat around the edges and then bake it for another 10 minutes.

5. Get the grapes ready by washing them, cutting them in half and placing them on a baking tray. Drizzle over the maple syrup and cinnamon, and then gently roast it in the oven at 280 degrees F for 15-20 minutes until caramelized.

6. Next, to make the cream, begin by creating an easy homemade creme patisserie. Gently warm the milk in a pan, being careful not to burn it. In a different bowl, add sugar, cornflour, egg yolks, egg, and vanilla. Whisk into a smooth paste.

7. When the mixture has become light and foamy, slowly pour it in the hot milk, whisking continuously to keep any lumps from forming. Once all the milk is mixed in, transfer it back into the pan and heat it for about 2-3 minutes, stirring continuously while it thickens. Transfer the mixture into a bowl, then cover with plastic wrap to keep a skin from forming and letting it cool.

8. For the grape jam filling, place a saucepan on medium heat and add in half of your caramelized grapes along with the sugar. Bring the mixture to a boil, breaking the grapes up as you stir them. After 5 minutes, transfer it to a food processor and blend it into your jam. Spread this over the bottom of the tart tin.

9. To finish up the cream, pour it into a bowl and whisk until it forms stiff peaks. Gently fold half the whipped cream into the cream patisserie, being careful not to knock out too much air. Then, when it's even, fold it in the remaining half of the cream. Transfer the cream into a piping bag to help distribute it evenly over the top of the grape filling.

10. Use the remaining grapes to decorate the top of your tart and use the red grapes to create the lightning bolt shape, lining it with the white grapes to help it stand out. Place the finished tart into the fridge for 30 minutes to firm.

Melon Sorbet

Servings: 8-12

Prep Time: 50 minutes, chill overnight

Cook Time: 0 minutes

Ingredients:

- 1 large honeydew melon

- 3.5 oz golden castor sugar

- 6.7 fl oz water

- 4 tbsp honey

- 1 lime (zest and juice)

- 3-4 sprigs of mint

Instructions:

1. Begin by preparing your fruit. Slice the melon in half lengthways, scoop out the seeds, and then slice the melon into cubes, using a spoon to scoop.

2. Next, place a pan on medium heat and add sugar, water, honey and melon, stirring it through until the mixture is even. While the mixture warms, grate the zest off the lime, squeeze out the juice, and add both into the syrup. Pull off the mint leaves and add those into the mixture as well. You can increase or decrease the amount according to your taste.

3. Allow it to simmer for ten minutes, then turn off the heat. Let the syrup infuse for five minutes to bring out the mint flavour, then transfer into a blender and beat until smooth.

4. Pour the syrup through a sieve and press it through to make sure you get an incredibly smooth sorbet. Pour the syrup into a bottle and refrigerate it until you are ready to use it.

5. For the best results use an ice cream machine. This normally needs to be chilled in the freezer overnight. The ice cream machine can create smaller ice crystals for a smooth finish. If you don't have one, you can simply use a plastic tub instead.

6. Prepare the ice cream machine and transfer the melon and mint syrup into it. Churn the mixture for 20 minutes until the sorbet has thickened. If you prefer a soft sorbet, you can serve it as is, or for a firmer sorbet, pour it into an ice cream tub, placing it in the freezer for an hour.

7. If you don't have an ice cream machine, pour the syrup into a tub and freeze it for 30 minutes. Remove the tub from the freezer and whisk it thoroughly. Return to the freezer for another 30 minutes and repeat the process until the sorbet has thickened.

8. Scoop the sorbet out into a glass or bowl and garnish it with finely chopped mint.

Cauldron Cakes

Servings: 10-12

Prep Time: 20 minutes

Cook Time: 15 minutes

Ingredients:

Spice Mix

- ½ tbsp ground cinnamon

- 1¼ tsp ground allspice

- ½ tsp ground nutmeg

- ¼ tsp ground ginger

- ¼ tsp ground anise

- ¼ tsp ground fennel seed

- ¼ tsp ground cloves

Cakes

- Canola oil spray

- 5.2-5.6 oz of pitted dates

- 1½ tsp of spice mix

- ½ tsp almond essence

- ½ cup white sugar

- 2 cups plain flour

- ½ cup butter, room temperature

- ¼ cup water

- Icing sugar for dusting

Instructions:

1. Preheat your oven to 350 degrees F.

2. Mix together the spice mix and place it into an airtight container as you'll only be using a little bit of the mix for the recipe.

3. Then, grease the blender with the canola oil, so the dates don't stick.

4. In batches, heat up the dates in a small microwavable bowl, microwaving for 10-15 seconds to soften them.

5. Place the dates in the food processor and blend. Repeat this process with the rest.

6. Using your hands, mix the 1 ½ teaspoon of spice mix and half a teaspoon of almond essence into the date mixture and set aside.

7. In the mixer, beat the butter, add in the sugar and beat it for a few minutes until it becomes creamy. Next, add in the flour, then the water.

8. Turn out the mixture onto a board dusted with plain flour and roll it out relatively thin. Now cut it into circles.

9. Spritz your cookie tray with canola oil spray and put one circle into a cookie hole.

10. Use a small ball of the date mixture, push it in with your fingers to make a flattened circle, and then place it into the cookie tray on top of the dough. Place another cookie dough circle on top. Push the center down, then press the edges together.

11. Redo this process, then place the tray into the oven to bake for 15-20 minutes, until golden brown. Then remove the tray from the oven, using

the back of a large spoon to push the middle in to keep the indentation gently, then set them aside to cool.

12. Dust them with icing sugar and serve.

Treacle Tart

Servings: 8

Prep Time: 20 minutes, 30 minutes chill time (dough)

Cook Time: 40 minutes

Ingredients:

● 2 sheets of frozen ready-made shortcrust pastry + 1 sheet if you want to decorate the top

● 2 lemons - juice and rind

● 1 cup Golden Syrup

● 4.9 oz white breadcrumbs

● 1 egg wash (optional)

Instructions:

1. Defrost the shortcrust pastry at room temperature or in the fridge as per the packet recommendations.

2. Preheat the oven to 320 degrees F.

3. Line a greased, 9-inch loose bottom tart pan with the pastry sheet. If one sheet isn't large enough, use an extra pastry sheet and gently press together to join them in the pan

4. Prick the base of the pastry case with a fork, then set it aside or chill it in the fridge if the room temperature is warm.

5. Make breadcrumbs by cutting off bread crusts and running them in the food processor until it's fine and fluffy.

6. Warm the Golden Syrup in a pan over low heat, adding lemon zest, lemon juice and breadcrumbs, then stir the mixture to combine.

7. Pour the filling into the pastry case and bake it for 45-60 minutes until set.

8. If you are adding pastry toppings, make a decorative lattice with a third sheet of pastry and add it on top of the filling about 20 minutes into the baking time.

9. Brush it with egg wash to assist with the browning.

10. Serve warm or cold with cream or ice cream.

Dessert for Breakfast

This dish pays homage to the traditional English Breakfast, with the twist that it consists entirely of sweet ingredients. With the intention to make the components imitate their savoury originals, it would make an ideal main dessert for any Hogwarts party and is sure to attract a lot of attention!

Servings: 2

Prep Time: 4-6 hours (including chill time)

Cook Time: 20-30 minutes

Ingredients:

Panna Cotta "Egg Whites"

- 1 gelatine leaf

- 2.5 oz milk

- 2.5 oz double cream

- ½ tsp vanilla extract

- 1 tbsp caster sugar

Orange Jelly "Egg Yolks"

- 1 gelatine leaf

- 5 fl oz smooth orange juice

Chocolate and Vanilla Sponge Cake

- 4 oz butter

- 4 oz golden castor sugar +1 tbsp

- 2 eggs

- ½ tsp vanilla extract

- ¼ tsp ground mixed spice

- ½ cup of self-raising flour

- 1 tbsp cocoa +1 tsp

- 2 tbsp buttercream icing

- 0.8 oz milk chocolate

- 0.8 oz white chocolate

Peach and Raspberry Jam and Marzipan "Beans"

- 1 ¼ cup of peaches

- ½ cups of raspberries

- ¾ cup of golden caster sugar

- 1.7 oz marzipan

Fondant "Bacon"

- 3.5 oz white fondant icing

- red, purple, and brown food colouring

- 1 tbsp cocoa

Instructions:

1. Begin with the parts that are going to take up the longest time to finish - Set the eggs. Then for the jelly yolks, bloom the gelatine by putting a gelatine sheet into a bowl of cold water and leaving it for 5 minutes until it's soft.

2. Heat the orange juice until it's hot, but don't boil it. Wring out the extra water from the gelatine and blend it into the juice.

3. Move the liquid into a jug and pour it into silicone sphere moulds about ½-inch in diameter. Then, place it in the fridge for at least 2 hours to set.

4. Duplicate these steps for the vanilla panna cotta. Blooming the gelatine leaf in cold water for five minutes, heating the milk, cream, vanilla, and sugar until it's warm in the meantime.

5. When the sugar has melted, press the surplus water out of the gelatine and mix it into the cream.

6. Spill the cream into a wide silicone dish, lining the dish with plastic wrap to make removal easier. Place the panna cotta into the fridge to set for two hours.

7. For the cake mix, use the all-in-one method by placing butter, sugar, eggs, mixed spice, vanilla, and flour into a bowl and beating it until smooth.

8. Take out around 6 tablespoons of cake mix and flavour it with your cocoa powder. This chocolate cake mix is for the sausages so that you can bake them in cupcake cases.

9. Oil a rectangular baking tin and line it with parchment paper before adding in the remaining cake mix. Smoothly lay out the mixture and then bake in the oven, along with the cupcakes, for ten to fifteen minutes at 350 degrees F. A skewer should come out clean when it's inserted into the cakes. Let it cool while you prepare the other ingredients.

10. Making the beans, you'll need to make the jam sauce by adding your peaches, raspberries, and sugar into a saucepan and bringing it to a boil.

11. Separate the fruit as it begins to soften and leave it to boil for 10 minutes until it's thick enough to coat the back of a spoon.

12. Place the fruit into a food processor and blend it until it's smooth. Then filter it through a colander to remove the seeds.

13. Divide the marzipan into pea-sized pieces, then fold it in your hand and pinch the middle to form a bean shape.

14. As soon as the jam has cooled, add a bit of orange juice to thin it down if it is too thick. Add in your marzipan beans and blend them through.

15. As soon as the cupcakes are cooled down, crumble the cake into a bowl and combine it with the buttercream. Press the mixture in your hands and mould it into sausage shapes.

16. Melt the chocolate and brush it over the chocolate sausages to get an even coat. Place them in the fridge until they've set.

17. To make the bacon, divide your icing into three, keep one white and colour the other one a dark red and a deeper reddish-purple. Marble these together and then shape the icing into a rectangle. Cut it up into strips.

18. Place some rods or pins on a board about ½-inch apart and lay your strips over the top, pressing them into the canals. Allow them to harden.

19. Mix some of your cocoa powder with hot water to create a paste and use this to make stripes on your chocolate sausages, as well as around the edges of your fondant bacon. Fade the cocoa with some paper towels, then take some plain cocoa and create definition along the sausages and over the bacon, paying attention to the grooves.

20. Now, take out the cooled vanilla sponge cake from the tin, slice it into two squares, and then slice them again diagonally for your toast slices. Sprinkle some sugar over the top, and then, using a blow torch, caramelize the top.

21. Put your Breakfast together by arranging the ingredients onto the plate or breakfast skillet. Shape the eggs by cutting out the shapes for the egg whites and then transfer them to the dish carefully. Then, using a spoon, place the yolks on top. If the panna cotta gets stuck, quickly dip the mould into hot water to loosen it.

Quidditch Cup-cakes

Servings: 30

Prep Time: 30 minutes

Cook Time: 15 minutes

Ingredients:

Lemon Cupcakes

- 3 cups all-purpose flour
- 2 tsp baking powder
- 1 tsp salt
- 1 cup unsalted butter, room temperature
- 2 cups granulated sugar
- 4 large eggs
- zest from 4 lemons
- ⅔ cup fresh lemon juice
- yellow food colouring, optional
- 1 cup buttermilk, room temperature
- 30 gold cupcake liners
- 5.25 oz gold sprinkles
- ½ (12 oz) bag white candy melts

Cream Cheese Frosting

- 16 oz cream cheese, cold

- 1 cup unsalted butter, room temperature

- 2 cups powdered sugar

- 2 tsp vanilla extract

Instructions:

1. Preheat the oven to 400 degrees F.

2. Whisk the flour, baking powder, and salt together in a large bowl and place it aside.

3. In the bowl of a stand mixer, cream the butter and sugar together with the paddle attachment. Next, add the eggs one at a time and mix thoroughly after each addition. Add the lemon zest, lemon juice, and a few drops of yellow food colouring (optional) and combine.

4. Alternate adding the flour mixture and buttermilk, beginning and ending with the flour mixture, but being careful not to overmix.

5. Line the muffin tins with thirty gold cupcake liners. Fill the cups two-thirds of the way full with batter.

6. Bake for 13-15 minutes or until cooked all the way through, then allow the cupcakes to rest for 10 minutes before moving them to cool on a wire rack.

7. Next, place the cream cheese in a mixing bowl and, using a hand mixer, beat until smooth. Gradually add the butter 2 tablespoons at a time, and continue beating until smooth and well blended.

8. Add powdered sugar and vanilla all at once and blend until combined and smooth. Be careful not to blend for too long as it will become too soft to pipe.

9. Melt the white candy melts according to the package directions and pour it into a Ziploc plastic bag, sealing it shut. Cut off the corner, then pipe wings onto a wax paper-lined cookie sheet.

10. Pipe a nice round button for the wing support, then the bottom feathers and a half circle for the top of the wing.

11. Place the wings in the fridge until it's set. Make sure you have at least sixty wings. Having some extra will come in handy if any wings break.

12. Place gold sprinkles in a large bowl, then fill a piping bag with an open coupler and the cream cheese frosting.

13. Pipe a dome on top of each cupcake by squeezing your piping bag close to the cupcake, directly in the center. Squeeze until the frosting almost reaches the edges and fills out into a nice round shape.

14. Immediately sprinkle the gold sprinkles over the frosting and on the sides until covered. Shake off any excess sprinkles. Repeat the process with each cupcake.

15. Place a left and right wing into the frosting of each cupcake and serve.

Cereal Treats

Servings: 12

Prep Time: 45 minutes

Cook Time: 0 minutes

Ingredients:

- 2 tbsp butter

- 3 cups mini marshmallows

- Red food colouring

- Green food colouring

- Yellow food colouring

- Blue food colouring

- 4 cups rice cereal treats, divided

- 5-6 oz yellow fondant

- 12 small paper wings

- Yellow decorating frosting

- Circular cookie cutter, about 2 inches in diameter

Instructions:

1. Line a baking pan with wax paper and set it aside.

2. Then, in a medium-sized saucepan, melt butter over medium heat and add in the marshmallows.

3. Stir the marshmallows until they are completely melted, being careful not to burn them.

4. When it has completely melted, remove it from heat and divide it into four separate bowls.

5. Add one colour to each bowl of marshmallows - about two to three small drops. Mix them together until they are completely tinted.

6. Fold in one cup of rice cereal treats into each bowl until all the ingredients are well combined.

7. Roll 1-inch spheres from each coloured rice cereal treat mixture. Place each sphere gently on a lined baking pan and allow the rice cereal treats to set for about 15 minutes.

8. Roll out the yellow fondant with a rolling pin until it's about a ¼-inch thick. Then, using the cookie cutter, cut out twelve yellow fondant circles.

9. Place one cereal treat in the center of a yellow fondant circle and stretch it over until the cereal treat is completely covered with fondant. Repeat this process for every rice cereal treat.

10. Place a small dot of yellow decorating frosting on the back of each set of paper wings, then place it on top of each covered rice cereal treat.

Golden Snitch Peanut Butter Balls

Servings: 12

Prep Time: 1 hour

Cook Time: 0 minutes

Ingredients:

- 1 cup peanut butter

- 3 cups powdered sugar

- 6 tbsp butter

- 1 cup yellow candy melts

- 8 dark cocoa candy melts

- 1 tsp vegetable oil

- Gold colour mist

- Gold glitter cardstock

- 24 toothpicks

- Mini squeeze bottle

Instructions:

1. Mix the peanut butter, butter, and powdered sugar in a bowl. Combine it until it's well blended and thick enough to form balls.

2. Make twelve peanut butter balls and place them on a cookie tray covered in parchment paper.

3. Place them in the fridge to set.

4. Combine yellow candy melts, dark cocoa candy melts, and vegetable oil in a separate bowl.

5. Microwave, stirring every 30 seconds until melted.

6. Remove the peanut butter balls from the refrigerator and dip them in the melted chocolate.

7. Place them back on wax paper and refrigerate again until the chocolate hardens. This will only take a few minutes.

8. Pour the leftover melted chocolate into a decorating bottle. The chocolate shells should be hardened around the peanut butter balls by now. Use the bottle to create Golden Snitch marlins on the peanut butter balls.

9. Mist the balls with gold colour mist and let them dry.

10. Cut wings from the gold card stock and glue the toothpicks to the back, keeping enough space free to stick into the ball.

11. Allow the colour to dry, then attach wings, and they are set to go.

12. Place it into the fridge until you are ready to serve.

CHAPTER VI

Dursley's in the Kitchen

Harry spent the first ten years of his life being raised by his Aunt Petunia and her family. Her husband, Vernon, and son, Dudley, had equally foul attitudes towards Harry during this time, making him sleep in a closet under the staircase at first and barely giving him anything to eat. While Dudley, on the other hand, received many wonderful foods and gifts from his parents, the picture of spoiled rotten.

The treats made by the Dursleys were always just out of reach for Harry, with them finding most occasions to indulge and leaving him with less. From savoury salmon dishes to a delicious Knickerbocker Glory, they made sure that every meal was irresistible. This led to Harry's food exploration during his stay at Hogwarts, and I have made sure to provide them here for everyone to enjoy.

Roasted Salmon with Feta and Herbs

Servings: 4

Prep Time: 5 minutes

Cook Time: 25 minutes

Ingredients:

- 2 ½ lbs salmon fillet, deboned
- 2 lbs asparagus, woody ends chopped off
- ⅔ cup feta cheese, crumbled
- ½ cup unsalted butter softened
- 2 tbsp fresh Italian parsley, chopped
- 1 tbsp fresh dill, chopped
- 1 tbsp fresh chives, chopped
- 2 tsp fresh oregano, chopped
- 1 tbsp garlic oil (or 2 cloves, minced)
- Zest of 1 lemon
- ¾ tsp sea salt
- Pepper to taste

Instructions:

1. Preheat the oven to 450 degrees F and prepare a baking sheet with parchment paper.

2. Transfer the asparagus to the baking tray in a flat row and lay the salmon fillet on top.

3. Reserve a small amount of herbs to the side and in a small bowl, mix the remainder of the herbs, garlic oil, lemon zest, and sea salt together, combining it with butter as well.

4. Spread mixture on top of the salmon until it is fully covered, then sprinkle it with feta and the reserved herbs. Finish it off with a few cracks of fresh black pepper.

5. Bake the dish for 25 minutes or until salmon has reached at least 140 degrees F.

6. Finish it under the broiler for 3-5 minutes or until the salmon has a little bit of crispy char on top.

Aunt Petunia's Pudding

Servings: 16

Prep Time: 2 hours

Cook Time: 1 hour

Ingredients:

- 8 eggs

- 2 cups + 2 tbsp caster sugar

- pinch of salt

- 4 tsp vanilla extract

- 3 tsp cornflour

- 1 ½ tsp white wine vinegar

- 5 cups of double cream

- 3 tbsp icing sugar

- green and purple food colouring

- 20 glace cherries

- edible violets

- white candy floss

Instructions:

1. Separate the egg whites carefully from the yolks, making sure the bowl is clean and free of grease. You can wipe the bowl with a lemon and paper towel to do this.

2. Whisk the egg whites on medium speed until it reaches soft peaks, then add in the sugar a spoonful at a time, waiting for it to be completely combined before adding more.

3. When the meringue turns glossy, add your salt, vanilla, cornflour and white wine vinegar and continue to whisk for about five minutes until it forms stiff peaks.

4. Use a round-bottomed tin to trace a circle onto your baking paper. Using two sizes, the large being 8 inches and three smaller circles of 6 inches.

5. Put the baking paper onto trays and transfer the meringue to a piping bag with a star nozzle. Pipe it around the circle stencil evenly and fill in the middle. Bake the discs in the oven at 212 degrees F for an hour and a half. Then turn off the oven and open the door slightly, leaving the meringue inside to cool off.

6. For the cream, stir in the food colouring, so you have 20 oz of green cream and 20 oz of purple. Whisk these with your vanilla and icing sugar until it forms stiff peaks; be careful not to over whip and place it in

piping bags. Transfer these bags to the fridge until the dish is ready to serve.

7. Clean the edible flowers. Then toss them in the castor sugar while they are still slightly wet and place them aside to dry.

8. Take a clear cake board and break off pieces of candy floss. Drape them around the sides to make it look like it's levitating on smoke, placing the largest meringue disc on top.

9. Begin the first layer alternately piping the purple and green cream around the outside, placing cherries on top of the green swirls and sugared violets on the purple swirls. Then fill the center of it with more cream.

10. Sandwich the next meringue disc over the center and alternate the cream as you stack the remaining layers. Large purple swirls with green in between, and then large green swirls with purple in between.

11. Lastly, for the top layer, you want to pipe continuous roses around the outside and place cherries in between.

Belgian Bun

Servings: 6

Prep Time: 40 minutes

Cook Time: 25 minutes

Ingredients:

- 1 cup of milk

- 1 sachet fast-action dried yeast

- 5 tbsp butter

- 1 egg

- 2 cups of plain flour

- zest of a lemon

- 3 tbsp sugar

- 1 tsp mixed spice

- 1 tsp vanilla

- 1 tsp salt

Filling

- 1 tbsp butter

- 1 tbsp sugar

- ½ tsp cinnamon

- 3.5 oz currants

Decoration

- 3.5 oz icing sugar

- 1 tbsp water

- ½ tbsp lemon juice

- 6 glace cherries

Instructions:

1. Warm the milk and butter in a saucepan and keep stirring until the butter has completely melted. Then place it aside.

2. Add in the flour, sugar, mixed spice, and lemon zest into a bowl and mix together until it's combined, making a shaft in the middle.

3. Pour the milk mixture into the middle and add your egg and vanilla extract and your salt and yeast; Add them on separate sides of the bowl to keep them from reacting to each other and mix into a dough. Knead the dough for about 5 minutes in a stand mixer, using a dough hook, or by hand for 10 minutes.

4. Oil up a bowl and place the pounded dough, cover it with plastic wrap and put in a heated area to rise for an hour until it's doubled in size.

5. When the dough is ready, knock it back by working for another minute and roll it out on a floured surface to about ½-inch thick.

6. Make the filling for the buns by melting your butter and stirring in your cinnamon and sugar. Brush this mixture over the rolled dough and sprinkle the currants on top. Press the currants in slightly to keep them in place.

7. Fold the dough along the length of it until it forms a long sausage. Then use a sharp knife to slice the roll into ½-inch wide buns, placing them onto a greased baking tray. Press each bun down slightly and wrap the tray in plastic wrap, letting the buns rise again for 45-60 minutes.

8. Brush the buns with a little milk and then bake in the oven at 350 degrees F for 15-20 minutes until they turn light and golden brown.

9. While the buns are cooling, make the frosting by mixing the icing sugar, water and lemon juice together. Scoop a few tablespoons over each bun and use a balanced spatula to smooth down the sides.

10. Lastly, cut up each cherry into fourths. Flatten the top of one fourth to create the top of the lightning bolt, then take another part and cut it diagonally from the bottom to create a point. Now, put them next to each other, and you should have a lightning bolt. Put them on top of your buns to finish.

Homemade Tea Bags

Aunt Petunia proves herself to be a formidable hostess and tries her best to cater to the needs and wants of her guests. This would be ideal for that book club meeting or a small gathering of kinds. With the flavours being made to suit the taste of each guest, it is sure to be a huge hit!

Servings: 20

Prep Time: 15 minutes

Cook Time: 2 hours (if dehydrating your own ingredients)

Ingredients:

- 20 tbsp loose leaf tea

- Juniper berries for Ravenclaw

- Cardamon for Slytherin

- Pink peppercorns for Gryffindor

- Hibiscus for Hufflepuff

- Disposable tea bags

- Assorted colour cards (for the tags)

Instructions:

1. Create your lightning bolt tags, snip your card into small pieces and then sketch your lightning bolts on top. Cut them out and pierce a hole in the top corner.

2. Get your disposable tea bags and fill them using a tablespoon of your choice of loose leaf tea. Next, add in a few of your flavours or botanicals.

3. Pull the tea bag closed and pull a string through the hole in your lightning bolts. Tie a knot to keep it securely in place and then cut off any excess parts.

4. Boil the kettle and place one tea bag into each mug. Then fill the mug three-quarters of the way up with hot water.

5. Let the tea brew for three to five minutes. The time you allow the tea to brew is all based on how strong you like it and then remove the tea-bag.

6. Add sugar, sweetener or milk to taste and serve it while it's hot.

Muggle-Friendly Fruit Cake

Servings: 12

Prep Time: 15 minutes

Cook Time: 2 hours

Ingredients:

- ¾ cup dark soft brown sugar

- ¾ cup caster sugar

- 1 cup butter

- 4 eggs

- 1 cup self-raising flour

- 1 tsp mixed spice

- 1 tsp vanilla extract

- 1 cup mixed fruits

- ¾ cup glace cherries

- 1 tbsp honey

- 1 tbsp hot water

Instructions:

1. Begin by adding the butter and sugar into a bowl and whisking it on a medium speed for 2-3 minutes until pale and fluffy. You can use half dark brown for the caramel flavour and half caster sugar for the texture.

2. Crack the eggs into a bowl and whisk them together until they are combined, mixing them into the butter and sugar after combining them a bit at a time. Use a spoonful of flour to bind the mixture if it begins to curdle.

3. Next, add in the flour, mixed spice and vanilla and then mix it on a slow speed until just combined.

4. Cut the cherries in half and then add them into the cake mix, along with the dried mixed fruits. Fold them through.

5. Grease and line a baking tray, and then spill in the cake batter using a spatula to level it off. Bake it in the oven at 350 degrees F for 35-40 minutes. It's ready once a skewer is inserted into the middle and comes out clean.

6. While the cake is still warm, mix the honey and hot water in a bowl and then generously brush over the top of the cake to give it a glossy finish.

Metropolitan Brandy Cocktail (Alcoholic)

Servings: 1

Prep Time: 5 minutes

Cook Time: 10-20 minutes

Ingredients:

- 2 fl oz brandy

- 1 fl oz vermouth

- ½ cup ice

- 1 tsp simple syrup

- 2-3 dashes Angostura bitters

- Ice

Instructions:

1. Make your simple syrup by adding equal parts of sugar and water into a saucepan. Half a cup of each will give you enough sugar syrup to keep in the fridge and make a variety of cocktails. Bring the syrup to boil until all the sugar has dissolved, and then set it to cool.

2. Place your cocktail glasses in the freezer to chill while preparing the drink.

3. The ratio of two parts brandy to one part vermouth will give you a perfectly balanced drink every time. Pour both spirits into your shaker and top it up with ice.

4. Add in your sugar syrup and Angostura bitters, placing the lid on top and shaking your cocktail for a minute or two.

5. Remove your cocktail glass from the freezer. You know they are appropriately chilled if they frost up while in contact with the room temperature air, then slowly pour your cocktail in using the strainer.

6. Garnish with a cherry.

7. Always drink responsibly.

Incredible Edible Cereal Bowl

Servings: 1

Prep Time: 60 minutes

Cook Time: 5 minutes

Ingredients:

- 1 oz butter

- 2 oz marshmallows

- ½ cup of preferred cereal

- ¼ cup of milk chocolate

- 3.5 oz white candy melts

- 1 ¼ cup of milk

Instructions:

1. Liquefy the butter and marshmallows in a bowl over simmering water and blend the mixture until it becomes smooth. Take it off of the heat and let it cool slightly.

2. Add the cereal into a mixing bowl, and then add the mixture of melted marshmallows on the top. Stir through entirely until all the cereal pieces are coated evenly.

3. Using plastic wrap, line a small bowl and then press an even layer of the cereal mixture around the sides of the bowl, filling the bottom last. To avoid the mixture sticking to your hands during this step, grease your hands with some oil or butter. Apply firm pressure to the mixture to make sure it holds its form and transfer it to the fridge to set for 10-15 minutes.

4. Next, melt the chocolate in a bowl over simmering water and remove the cereal bowl from the fridge. Then, using a silicone brush, spread the chocolate on the inside of the bowl. You'll need to paint about three layers to keep the milk from spilling out. Place the chocolate covered cereal in the freezer and flash-freeze it for 5 minutes. Repeat this step with more chocolate to make sure the bowl is sealed properly.

5. Melt the candy melts in the microwave or a bowl over simmering water, and then place them into a piping bag with a writing tip.

6. You need to work fast before the candy melts set, pipe out splash shapes onto some baking paper, make two sides for each of the 3D splashes and place them into the fridge for 10 minutes to set.

7. Remove the cereal bowl from the mould. Put a little bit of melted white candy melts into the bottom of the cereal bowl and, on each side, stick together the milk splashes, holding them to the side of the bowl long enough until they stay in place. To create a dripping effect, drizzle some of the leftover candy melts over the milk splashes. Place it back in the fridge for five minutes to set.

8. When it's ready, slowly pour in your milk. To create the illusion of a full bowl, add in more cereal on the top.

Knickerbocker Glory Ice Cream Sundae

Servings: 1

Prep Time: 20-30 minutes

Cook Time: 0 minutes

Ingredients:

- 1 cup mixed fresh fruit

- 2 scoops of vanilla ice cream

- 2 tbsp fruit syrup

- ¼ cup whipping cream

- 1 tbsp dark chocolate chips

Instructions:

1. Whip the whipping cream to a soft peak consistency.

2. Take two tall glasses and add mixed chopped fruit into both glasses, leaving some for another layer.

3. Add in the ice cream and drizzle syrup over it.

4. Top with some chopped fresh fruit, whipped cream, chocolate chips, and serve.

CHAPTER VII

A Buttery Delight

Buttered Brew

This is probably the most well-known part of the wizarding universe. This famous brew has been making an appearance in many new shapes and forms. Buttered beer can be served hot and foaming in a mug, but also bottled and cold. The Three Broomsticks Inn attempted to make a sweeter version of this drink and was met with great reviews. Wizard or non-wizards alike, this drink is addictively delicious.

Servings: 4

Prep Time: 10 minutes

Cook Time: 50 minutes

Ingredients:

- 1 cup light or dark brown sugar

- 2 tbsp water

- 6 tbsp butter

- ½ tsp salt

- ½ tsp cider vinegar

- ¾ cup heavy cream, divided

- ½ tsp rum extract

- 4 (12 oz) bottle cream soda

Instructions:

1. Using a small saucepan, place it over medium heat, pour in the brown sugar and water and bring it to a gentle boil, stirring it occasionally until the temperature reaches 240 degrees F (use a sugar thermometer).

2. Add in the butter, salt, vinegar and a quarter of the heavy cream, stirring it as you add it in. Put it aside and let it cool to room temperature.

3. Stir in your rum extract when the mixture has cooled down.

4. Combine two tablespoons of the brown sugar mixture in a medium bowl with the remaining half cup of heavy cream. Using an electric mixer, beat the mixture until it just starts to thicken for about 2-3 minutes, but don't whip it completely.

5. Divide the mixture into four tall glasses, add a quarter cup of cream soda to each glass, and stir it to combine it. Fill the glasses with extra cream soda until the glass is nearly filled to the top, then top it off with a spoon full of whipped cream.

Buttered Brew Porridge

Servings: 4

Prep Time: 15 minutes

Cook Time: 35 minutes

Ingredients:

- 2 cups of oats (½ cup per person)

- 4.2 cups of milk (1 cup per person)

- pinch of salt

- ½ tsp nutmeg

- 1 tsp vanilla

- 1 tbsp sugar

Butterscotch Sauce

- 3 ½ oz light brown sugar

- 1 ½ fl oz water

- 0.8 oz butter

- 1 ¼ cup of double cream

- 1 tsp vanilla

- pinch of salt

Instructions:

1. Start preparing the butterscotch sauce by placing sugar and water in a pan and bringing the mixture to a boil. Let it caramelize until it turns a dark golden brown, and avoid stirring it too much. Just swirl the mixture in the pan to help the sugar dissolve.

2. Add in the butter and whisk until melted, adding in the cream slowly afterwards as you stir it until smooth. The mixture may bubble and spit, so be careful. Add in vanilla and salt to flavour, and then pour it into a bowl to let it cool.

3. To make the porridge, add oats, milk, salt, nutmeg and vanilla into a pot and stir it on medium heat for 4-5 minutes. Keep mixing it to keep it from burning. It should thicken as well.

4. Take out two large scoops of porridge for topping and place it into a bowl. Flavour it with sugar. Mixing the additional porridge with the butterscotch sauce.

5. Fill the mugs to about half an inch from the top with the porridge mixture, and then spoon the white porridge over the top.

6. Dust some nutmeg and serve it hot.

Buzzing Butterscotch Milkshake

Servings: 4

Prep Time: 10 minutes

Cook Time: 0 minutes

Ingredients:

- 2 cup double cream + 1 ¼ cup
- 1 can condensed milk
- pinch of salt
- 2-3 tbsp caramel extract
- 3 ½ oz light brown sugar
- 1 ½ fl oz water
- 0.8 oz butter
- 1 tsp vanilla
- pinch of salt
- 1.7 oz white chocolate
- 4 tbsp butterscotch sauce
- 6 scoops of butterbeer ice cream
- 1 ½ cup of milk (depending on the thickness)
- Squirty cream
- Toppings of choice

Instructions:

1. Start by whisking 2 cups of double cream until it forms soft peaks, then add in the condensed milk, vanilla, caramel and salt and keep on whisking the mixture until it forms stiff peaks. Move to an ice cream tub and place it in the freezer for 4 hours or overnight (recommended).

2. Prepare the butterscotch sauce by placing your sugar and water in a pan and bringing the mixture to a boil. Let it caramelize until it turns a dark golden brown, and avoid stirring it too much. Just swirl the mixture in the pan to help the sugar dissolve. Add in the butter and whisk it until melted, adding the rest of the double cream slowly as you stir until smooth. The mixture may bubble and spit, so be careful. Add in vanilla and salt to flavour, and then pour it into a bowl to let it cool.

3. Melt the white chocolate in a bowl over simmering water until it becomes smooth, and then dip the rim of your glasses in and then turn it upside down, leaving the drips to run. You can then add more around the edge with a spoon, also adding in some of the cooled, thickened butterscotch sauce.

4. For the milkshake, add the ice-cream, butterscotch sauce, and milk into a blender and blend it together until smooth. Use a cocktail shaker if a blender is not available.

5. Pour the milkshake into the glasses you prepared and leave about half an inch open at the top. Finish off with a swirl of whipped cream on the top and your favourite candies or chocolates to garnish. Serve cold.

Babbling Charm Blondie

Servings: 16

Prep Time: 10 minutes

Cook Time: 50 minutes

Ingredients:

- 2 cups flour
- ½ tsp baking soda
- ¾ tsp baking powder
- 1 cup butter, softened
- 1 ½ cups of brown sugar
- ½ cup granulated sugar
- 1 egg
- 3 tbsp caramel sauce
- ½ tsp vanilla extract
- 2 ½ cups of butterscotch chips
- ½ cup powdered sugar
- 3 tbsp milk

Instructions:

1. Preheat your oven to 325 degrees F.

2. Spray a 9x13-inch baking pan with cooking spray.

3. Using a medium bowl, whip the flour, baking soda, and baking powder together.

4. Then, using a large bowl, whisk together the butter and sugars until the mixture is combined.

5. Place the eggs into the bowl and beat it for one minute.

6. Whisk in the caramel and vanilla.

7. Slowly add in the dry ingredients until it is just combined.

8. Stir in the butterscotch chips using a rubber spatula.

9. Spread the batter evenly into a prepared baking dish.

10. Bake the batter for 40-50 minutes until a knife inserted in the center comes out mostly clean, and the top has turned golden brown.

11. Move the baking dish to the top of a wire rack and leave it to cool entirely before cutting it into bars.

12. Whisk the powdered sugar and the milk together until it forms the desired consistency.

13. Drizzle the icing over the bars and serve.

Butterscotch Chip Cookies

Servings: 36

Prep Time: 2 hours 15 minutes

Cook Time: 10 minutes

Ingredients:

- 1 cup butter or margarine, softened

- 1 cup sugar

- 1 cup brown sugar

- 2 large eggs

- 1 tsp vanilla

- 1 tsp. salt

- 1 tsp baking soda

- 1 (5.1 0z) box butterscotch pudding

- 2 ¾ cup flour

- 1 cup butterscotch chips

- 1 cup white chocolate chips

Instructions:

1. Preheat the oven to 375 degrees F. Combine your butter or margarine and both sugars in the stand mixer using the paddle attachment. Then add in your eggs and vanilla.

2. Whisk the salt, baking soda, and pudding together in a different bowl and add to the wet mixture. Slowly pour in the flour.

3. Add on the chocolate chips and, with a wooden spoon, mix it in thoroughly. Cover the mixture and place it in the fridge for 15-20 minutes to chill.

4. Bake the batter on a greased baking sheet for 7-9 minutes, or until it turns a light golden brown on top. Place it onto a cooling rack to cool and enjoy.

Butterscotch Caramel Popcorn

Servings: 12

Prep Time: 15 minutes

Cook Time: 15 minutes

Ingredients:

- 12 cups air-popped popcorn

- 1 tsp baking soda

- ¼ tsp ground nutmeg

- 4 tsp pure vanilla extract

- 1 tsp almond extract

- 1 tsp butter flavouring

- ¾ tsp rum flavouring

- 8 tbsp unsalted butter

- 1 cup sugar

- 3 tbsp blackstrap molasses

- 1 tbsp water

- ½ tsp coarse kosher salt (use less if using fine salt)

Instructions:

1. Place the popcorn into a large bowl and put it aside. Take a large baking sheet and line it with parchment paper, and set it aside. Then sift together nutmeg, baking soda and cloves into a small bowl. Place this aside as well. Add the vanilla extract, almond extract, butter extract, and rum extract to a small bowl and place it aside.

2. Now, cook the butter, sugar, molasses, water, and salt in a medium, heavy-bottomed saucepan over medium heat and let the temperature rise until it reaches 305 degrees F, stirring the mixture occasionally. Carefully stir in the mixture of extracts and then the baking soda and spice mix. Pour the toffee over the popcorn and nut mixture.

3. Using two heat-safe rubber spatulas, jumble the popcorn around to spread the toffee throughout. Then spread the popcorn out onto the prepared baking sheet.

4. Allow the popcorn to cool and then break it apart.

Buttered Beere in a Mug

Servings: 1

Prep Time: 15 minutes

Cook Time: 2-3 minutes

Ingredients:

- ⅓ cup of flour

- ¼ cup sugar

- ¼ tsp baking powder

- ⅛ tsp salt

- ¼ cup buttermilk

- 1 tsp cream soda

- ½ tsp vanilla extract

- 2 tbsp melted butter

Butterbeer Frosting

- 3 cups powdered sugar

- 8 oz (2 sticks or 1 cup) unsalted butter, at room temperature

- ¼ tsp salt

- 2 tsp vanilla extract

- 2 tbsp milk

- 2 tbsp butterscotch syrup

Instructions:

1. Add the cake ingredients to a bowl and mix them together until it's smooth.

2. Spray a glass mug with cooking spray and pour the cake batter into the mug. Bake it in the microwave for 2 minutes and 15 seconds.

3. Let the cake cool and make the flavoured frosting by mixing the powdered sugar, butter, salt, vanilla, milk, and butterscotch syrup together.

4. The cake with frosting or scoop out a spoonful of cake and layer it, ensuring you end with the last layer as frosting.

5. Drizzle some syrup over the top before serving.

Buttered Brew Fudge

Servings: 64

Prep Time: 10 minutes

Cook Time: 15 minutes

Ingredients:

Bottom Layer

- 3 cups butterscotch chips

- 1 can condensed milk

- ½ cup powdered sugar

- ¼ cup butter

- ¼ tsp rum extract

- ½ tsp butter extract

Top Layer

- 1 ½ cups white chocolate chips

- 2 tbsp butter

- ½ can of condensed milk

- ¼ cup powdered sugar

- ¼ tsp vanilla

Instructions:

1. Get a 9x9-inch pan ready with wax paper or tin foil.

2. Using a large microwave-safe bowl, mix the butterscotch chips and butter together, heating it in the microwave for 1 minute and stirring it until smooth. Keep heating it in 15-second intervals if needed and stir in the milk, powdered sugar and extracts.

3. Pour the mixture into the prepared pan and put it in the freezer for 30 minutes to start with the set up.

4. In a separate microwave-safe bowl, mix the white chocolate chips and butter together. Heat it in the microwave for 1 minute and stir until smooth. If needed, keep heating it in 15-second intervals and stir in the milk, powdered sugar, and vanilla.

5. Let it cool slightly and then pour gently over the top of the first layer. Then place it in the fridge to set.

6. Cut into bite-sized pieces and serve.

CHAPTER VIII

The Headmaster's Ideal Meal

A secret organization was created by Harry, Hermione, and Ron dubbed Dumbledore's Army. They started this initiative to teach their fellow students proper techniques for Defense Against the Dark Arts. Hermione was the original founder, but Harry led the students and was also responsible for the lessons they took part in. This movement was needed due to Dolores Umbridge. She refused to teach anything other than theory in her classes, causing the students to rebel and to practice their magical skills in secret. There were a total of twenty-eight members.

However, the group broke up when Snape took over the teaching position of Defense Against the Dark Arts. This movement was restarted during Lord Voldemort's take-over by Neville, Ginny and Luna. They played an important role in the Second Wizarding War, the members taking part in numerous historical battles. One thing is certain though, this must have been hard and hungry work! The students needed food that would not only boost their morale but would recharge them. We also can't forget the Headmaster's favourite treat: Lemon Sherbet!

Mushroom and Lentils Stew

Servings: 4

Prep Time: 10 minutes

Cook Time: 20 minutes

Ingredients:

- 1 tbsp oil

- 2 shallots minced

- 2 cloves of garlic minced

- 1 ½ cup mushrooms diced

- 1 cup beer (dark beer provides a stronger flavour)

- 1 cup water

- ½ tsp salt

- 2 tsp maple syrup

- 1 tsp thyme

- ¼ tsp ground black pepper

- ½ cup dry green lentils

- 1 large carrot, peeled and cut into thin slices

- 1 large white potato, peeled and diced

- ⅓ cup green peas

- fresh parsley

- biscuits or bread for serving

Instructions:

1. Using a cast iron saucepan, heat the oil and add in the shallots and garlic. Sauté for about 5 minutes until the shallots are golden brown.

2. Then add the diced mushrooms and sauté for another 5 minutes, stirring it frequently. Deglaze it with the beer and let it simmer for another 5 minutes.

3. Now add in the water, salt, maple syrup, thyme, black pepper, green lentils, carrot, potato, and green peas.

4. Place a lid over the top and let simmer for about 30 minutes until the lentils and potatoes are tender. Top it with fresh parsley and serve with buttermilk biscuits or bread on the side.

Scottish Porridge

Servings: 4

Prep Time: 14 minutes

Cook Time: 12 minutes

Ingredients:

- 1 cup Scottish oats

- 1 ½ cups milk

- 1 ½ cups of water

- ½ tsp ground nutmeg

- ½ tsp ground cinnamon

- ¼ tsp sea salt

- ½ tsp vanilla (optional)

Instructions:

1. Place a pot on medium to high heat, bring oats, milk, water, and salt to a simmer.

2. When the oats begin to simmer, bring the heat down to medium to low and let it cook for 5-7 minutes, stirring it now and then. The mixture must have started thickening around this time.

3. Add in nutmeg, cinnamon, and vanilla, stirring it to combine the ingredients.

4. Cook for an extra minute or two until the porridge is thick but can still be poured.

5. Take it off of the heat, letting it cool for a few minutes, allowing the porridge to thicken even more.

6. Serve the dish with your favourite toppings.

Home Roasted Coffee

Servings: Depends on the amount of coffee beans you want

Prep Time: 1-2 hours

Cook Time: 10-15 minutes

Ingredients:

- raw (green) coffee beans

Instructions:

1. Using a clean cast iron skillet, place it on medium to high heat. Any greasiness on the skillet will affect the roast quality.

2. Add a layer of the coffee beans into the skillet, checking that you don't add too much and allowing space for the beans to keep moving as it heats up.

3. Keep moving them as they roast. You should start hearing cracks as they lose moisture inside. This process can take around 10-15 minutes. Should you notice the bean changing colour too quickly, turn down the heat.

4. Roast them to the colour you prefer and move them over to a bowl to allow them to cool off before handling.

5. Using a grinder, grind your coffee beans, or if you don't have one, blitz them in a food processor to the consistency of your choosing. You can also use a blender if you do not have a coffee grinder.

6. To make cold brew, place two tablespoons of the coffee powder into the brewer and fill it with water. Then place it in the fridge for a minimum of 12 hours.

Firewhisky Eggnog (Alcoholic)

Servings: 4-6

Prep Time: 20 minutes

Cook Time: 8 minutes

Ingredients:

- 3 eggs

- 1.7 oz golden caster sugar

- 1.7 oz light brown sugar

- 6 fl oz milk

- 8 ½ oz double cream

- 6 oz Firewhisky (See Chapter 10)

- 2-3 dashes Angostura bitters

- Nutmeg to taste

Instructions:

1. Separate the yolks of the egg from the egg whites and place them in an airtight container, storing them for later.

2. Using a bowl, put the egg yolks over simmering water, adding in your two sugars and whisk them together for about 5 minutes until it begins to turn pale, light, and frothy.

3. Take it off from the heat and whisk in your milk slowly, then add in the cream, bitters and firewhisky. When the base has become smooth, flavour it with nutmeg to taste. The firewhisky can also be replaced with a vanilla sugar syrup, which can be made by simply heating the sugar

from this recipe with 3 fl of water and 1 teaspoon of vanilla until it begins to boil. Let the mixture cool before using it.

4. When the base has become smooth, add in nutmeg to taste.

5. When ready to serve the drink, you can pasteurize the egg whites by placing them in a bowl over simmering water, whisk them lightly for 5 minutes until they are warm and frothy, and when they can form stiff peaks.

6. Pour the eggnog base into a separate jug and add a third of the egg whites. Stir to loosen and add in the second third. Fold these thoroughly to make sure they have combined evenly. Fold in the last third of the egg whites to finish it off.

7. Pour the eggnog into a serving glass and sprinkle some nutmeg over the top as garnish.

Lemon Sherbet

Servings: 10-12 sweets

Prep Time: 1 hour

Cook Time: 30-45 minutes

Ingredients:

Foam Sweet Layer

- 2 gelatine leaves

- 1.7 oz sugar

- 2 ½ oz water

- 1.7 oz glucose syrup

- ½ tsp vanilla

- 1 tbsp icing sugar

- 1 tbsp cornflour

Sherbet Lemon Jelly

- 8 gelatine leaves

- 5 oz lemon juice and zest (from fresh lemons)

- 3 ½ oz sugar

- ½ tsp citric acid

- yellow food colouring (optional)

Sherbet Lemon Coating

- 1.7 oz sugar

- ½ tsp citric acid

Instructions:

1. Create the sweet gummy foam by blooming your gelatine leaves in cold water, setting it aside for 5 minutes until they are soft.

2. Making a sugar syrup, place sugar, water and glucose syrup on a pan and over medium heat. Swirl the mixture and place a sugar thermometer in, letting it boil to the "softball" stage at 240 degrees F.

3. As soon as the syrup reaches the right temperature, take it off of the heat. Then take the gelatine out of the water and squeeze it to remove the extra water. Add it into the sugar syrup, stirring it until it dissolved. Move the mixture over to a bowl and whisk it on high speed for about 3 minutes until stiff peaks begin to form. Adding in vanilla, keep whisking for another 2 minutes.

4. Mix in cornflour and icing sugar together, coating the inside of a lemon wedge to keep it from sticking. Put the marshmallow foam in a piping bag with a writing tip and pipe the "rind" around the bottom of the mould, working quickly to keep the foam layer from becoming too thick while you work. Put it aside so it can become firm for about 15 minutes, prepare the jelly in the meantime.

5. Place the gelatin in cold water and let it bloom for 5 minutes to become soft. While you wait, start grating off the rind of the lemons and squeeze out the juice. Make this process easier by rolling the lemons on the counter to soften them up before you cut them.

6. Place a pan on medium heat and add in the lemon zest and juice, also putting in sugar and citric acid. Bring the mixture to a boil, then switch the heat off to keep the mix from evaporating.

7. It is optional, but you can add in your yellow food colouring and then squeeze out the extra water from your gelatin leaves and add in the lemon syrup, stirring it to blend the mixture well.

8. Pour the mixture into a jug and then pour your jelly into the moulds, starting off with only filling it halfway with jelly, freezing it for 10 minutes and then adding the remaining amount. This is to keep the foam from floating. Then place your mould into the fridge and let your jelly sweets set for 2 hours.

9. Make the lemon coating by adding the sugar and citric acid together and mixing them until they are blended completely. Gently take the jelly candy out of the moulds, dipping its base in hot water to make the process easier and quicker. It should be possible to slide them out easily with your spatula.

10. Prepare the coating by mixing the citric acid and sugar together. Then throw the jelly candies into the coating, be sure to cover them entirely and then place them on a plate to serve.

CHAPTER IX

Pick Your Potions

One of the more important classes young wizards and witches must attend is Potions. Just like you follow specific recipes to create delicious dishes, they do the same to create wondrous potions with otherworldly results. This is one of the key classes in the curriculum of a young student in Hogwarts, and it is expected to become standard knowledge as the student takes on adult life in the world of wizardry.

Potions in the muggle world aren't quite the same as the elixirs that are mixed within the magical realm. They consist of more attainable ingredients, and the effects are a little different and less potent. Some are intended for adults only, while the whole family can enjoy some.

Felix Felicis (Alcoholic)

Servings: 1 shot

Prep Time: 3 minutes

Cook Time: 0 minutes

Ingredients:

- 0.6 fl oz Lillet Blanc

- 0.5 fl oz Lychee Liqueur

- 0.3 fl oz Cointreau

- 1 bar spoon Luxardo Maraschino Liqueur

- 1 drop Gold Luster Gel

Instructions:

1. Add all the ingredients into a mixer with a single ice cube. Stir to combine and chill before straining into a shot glass.

Skele-Gro

Servings: 4-6

Prep Time: 20-30 minutes

Cook Time: 0 minutes

Ingredients:

- 1 small papaya

- 3 passion fruits

- 3 ½ oz dates (pitted)

- 3 bananas

- 1.7 oz goji berries

- 7 oz greek yogurt (with added vitamin D if you can find it)

- 17 fl oz milk

Instructions:

1. Peel the skin off the papaya and slice it in half, lengthwise, then use a spoon to scoop out the seeds and chop the papaya into small chunks.

2. Slice the passion fruits in half and then scoop out the insides, throwing away the skin.

3. Next, chop the pitted dates into small chunks. If you couldn't find seedless dates, slice the dates you have in half and remove the pit.

4. Peel the bananas and chop them into small chunks as well.

5. Put all the fruit into the blender, along with the goji berries, yogurt and milk and then blend them until they become thick and smooth.

6. Do a taste test, and add more milk if the potion is too thick.

7. Transfer the potion into a jug and seal tightly with a lid. It will last for three days in the fridge.

8. Serve the potion cold, shaking it well before pouring it into a glass.

Polyjuice Potion

Servings: 4-6

Prep Time: 20-30 minutes

Cook Time: 0 minutes

Ingredients:

- 3 ½ oz spinach

- 3 ½ oz kale

- 2 kiwis

- 1 slice of ginger

- 1 lime

- 17 oz pineapple juice

Instructions:

1. Prepare your fruit and vegetables by chopping any large stems off the spinach and kale and then wash them thoroughly to make sure they are clean.

2. Peel the skin off the kiwi and then chop it into rough chunks. Repeat the process with the ginger, peeling off the skin and chopping it into pieces.

3. Zest the lime before slicing it into halves and squeezing the juice out.

4. Add all of the ingredients into the blender with the pineapple juice and blend it until it becomes thick and smooth.

5. Taste the smoothie, adding more pineapple juice if it is too thick and more lime if it is too sweet, or more ginger if you want it a bit spicier.

6. When you are happy with the flavour, pour it into a jug and secure it tightly with a lid. You can refrigerate this for 3-4 days.

7. Fill a glass with ice, shake the bottle of Polyjuice and then quickly pour it over the ice. The air pockets between the ice should make your Polyjuice Potion bubble.

Pepper-Up Potion

Servings: 5-6

Prep Time: 15-20 minutes

Cook Time: 45-60 minutes

Ingredients:

- 4 cloves garlic

- 3 ½ oz - 5 oz ginger root

- 1 tbsp turmeric

- 1 lemon

- 2-3 tbsp honey

- 34 fl oz water

Instructions:

1. Peel the garlic and ginger, chop them into rough chunks and then run in a food processor. Add these ingredients into a pan on medium heat, add turmeric, and fry it for 3-5 minutes to cook off the spices.

2. Zest and juice your lemons and then add both ingredients into the pan, stirring through to remove any spices off the bottom.

3. Add in your honey with your water and let it boil.

4. When the mixture is bubbling, bring the heat down to low and put on the lid. Leave it to simmer for 30 minutes to bring out more of the flavour.

5. To make the mixture extra strong, pour it into a blender and mix it until it's nice and smooth. For a mild to medium flavour, pour the potion through a sieve to remove the garlic and ginger.

6. When it has cooled, you can bottle the potion up and keep it in the fridge for 3-5 days.

7. To get most of the health benefits, serve the beverage hot by warming it in a pan or in the microwave.

Homemade Firewhisky

Servings: 4-6 drinks

Prep Time: 20 minutes (1 month to infuse)

Cook Time: 30 minutes

Ingredients:

Firewhisky

- 17 oz whisky

- 1-2 whole chillies

- 2 cinnamon sticks

Simple Syrup

- 4 tbsp sugar

- 4 tbsp water

- chillies and cinnamon from firewhisky

Spicy Pumpkin Cocktail

- 1.6 oz Firewhisky

- 1.6 oz Pumpkin Juice

- 1 tbsp lemon juice

- 1 tbsp chilli simple syrup

- A few dashes Angostura Bitters

- Ice to serve

- Cinnamon and chilli to garnish

Instructions:

1. Cut up your chillies in half and put them into your bottle of whisky. Let this mature for a month, giving it a lot of time to allow the flavour to infuse with the whisky. You may leave it to infuse for more time or less time, depending on the intensity of the flavour you want. Remember that the chillies add heat, while cinnamon adds a spicy-sweet taste.

2. Filter the whiskey through a colander and taste test to ensure you are satisfied with the flavour. Rebottle, and if you would like to add more flavour, repeat step one and leave for a little longer.

3. To make the Spicy Pumpkin cocktail, make simple chilli syrup by placing sugar, water, chillies and cinnamon into a pan on medium heat and swirl it around until the sugar has dissolved. When the syrup has started bubbling, remove it from the heat and place the mixture in a bottle. Keep it in the fridge for three to four days.

4. Fill the shaker with ice and top it off with your firewhisky, pumpkin juice, lemon juice, chilli syrup, and Angostura bitters. Put on a lid and shake for 30 seconds.

5. Fill your serving glass to the top with ice, then add in the Spicy Pumpkin over the top, and using extra chilis and a cinnamon stick, garnish the drink and serve.

Simple Syrup

Making this syrup before starting off with the next few cocktails will save you some time in preparing the following cocktails.

Servings: 4

Prep Time: 5 minutes

Cook Time: 30 minutes

Ingredients:

- ½ cup sugar

- ½ cup water

Instructions:

1. Using a saucepan, add in the sugar and water and place it onto medium heat until it just starts to bubble and the sugar has completely dissolved.

2. Let it cool entirely before using.

Campari Spritz for Gryffindor (Alcoholic)

Servings: 1

Prep Time: 5 minutes

Cook Time: 0 minutes

Ingredients:

- 2 oz Campari

- 1 oz soda water

- 2 oz prosecco

- Ice

- Orange (garnish)

Instructions:

1. Fill up your glass with ice and pour in your Campari and soda water. Stir it together until mixed well.

2. Top up the rest of the glass with ice and pour in the prosecco

3. Use an orange slice to garnish.

Classic Margarita for Slytherin (Alcoholic)

Servings: 1

Prep Time: 5 minutes

Cook Time: 0 minutes

Ingredients:

- 2 oz tequila of choice

- 0.6 oz triple sec

- 0.5 oz simple syrup

- 1 oz fresh lime juice

- Lime wedges and salt (to garnish)

- Ice

Instructions:

1. Place the ice into your cocktail mixer, as well as your tequila, triple sec, sugar syrup and lime juice.

2. Place the outer edge of the glass in some lime juice and then dip it into salt and top it up with ice.

3. Shake it well for one minute, and then pour the drink into your glass. Garnish the drink with a lime wedge before you serve it.

Blue Lagoon for Ravenclaw (Alcoholic)

Servings: 1

Prep Time: 3 minutes

Cook Time: 0 minutes

Ingredients:

- 1 oz vodka of choice

- 1 oz blue curacao

- 4 oz lemonade

- Orange and cherries (to garnish)

- ice

Instructions:

1. Place the ice into your cocktail mixer and put in your vodka and blue curacao. Put the lid on top and shake it properly.

2. Load up the glass with ice and pour the blue mixture over it, then top with lemonade and garnish the drink with your orange peel and cherries on a cocktail stick.

Amaretto Spritz for Hufflepuff (Alcoholic)

Servings: 1

Prep Time: 5 minutes

Cook Time: 0 minutes

Instructions:

- 2 oz amaretto of choice

- 1 oz lemon juice

- 1 tbsp egg white

- Few dashes of Angostura bitters

- Cherries (to garnish)

- Ice

Instructions:

1. Fill your shaker with ice and then pour in your amaretto, lemon juice, egg white and bitters.

2. Shake the ingredients well for two minutes until the drink has turned pale in colour and has frothed up.

3. Lastly, jam your glass with ice and pour the cocktail over it. Leave it to stand for thirty seconds to let the froth form, and then garnish the drink with cherries on a cocktail stick.

Amortentia Potion (Alcoholic)

Servings: 2

Prep Time: 5 minutes

Cook Time: 0 minutes

Ingredients:

- 0.8 oz Amaretto of choice

- 1.6 oz gin of choice

- 1.6 oz triple sec

- 2 tbsp lemon juice

- 3 oz cranberry juice

- Ice

- Edible glitter

- Soda water or lemonade to finish

- Goji berries to garnish

Instructions:

1. Fill your cocktail shaker halfway with ice and add in the amaretto, gin, and triple sec over the top.

2. Roll a lemon on a worktop, cut it in half, and squeeze out the juice—strain to remove any seeds and add 2 tablespoons into the cocktail shaker. Then pour in the cranberry juice and place the lid on top.

3. Shake the cocktail base for a minute until the shaker is frosted, then you can decide whether to use the mixture immediately or if you would rather place it in a bottle and store it for later.

4. Serve the drink by filling the glass with ice and pour the cocktail carefully down the side of the glass until it is an inch from the top, keeping the top of the ice as dry as possible. Carefully pour the cocktail base down the side of the glass until it's an inch from the top, keeping the top of the ice as dry as possible.

5. Lastly, sprinkle the edible glitter over the top of the ice. Just before serving the drink, pour soda water, or lemonade if you prefer a sweeter taste, over the top and swirl the glitter into the drink. Add berries to garnish.

Gilly Water

Servings: 1 pitcher

Prep Time: 30 minutes

Cook Time: 0 minutes

Ingredients:

- 1-gallon water

- ½ large cucumber, spiralized

- 3 sprigs fresh mint

- Ice

Instructions:

1. Layer the ice, mint, and cucumber in a pitcher.

2. Pour the water into the prepared pitcher.

3. Place it in the fridge for 30-60 minutes

4. Add more ice if needed and serve.

Draught of Living Death (Alcoholic)

Servings: 2

Prep Time: 5 minutes

Cook Time: 0 minutes

Ingredients:

- 2 oz cranberry juice

- 1 oz blue curacao

- 1 oz vodka

- 1 oz rum

- 1 oz gin

- 6 oz tonic water or soda water, chilled

- 1 cup crushed ice

Instructions:

1. Using a cocktail shaker with ice, mix together the cranberry juice, blue curacao, vodka, rum, and gin.

2. Pour the mixture between two glasses of finely ice, then top it off with a chilled water mixer of choice.

Dementor's Kiss (Alcoholic)

Servings: 4

Prep Time: 30 minutes

Cook Time: 10 minutes

Ingredients:

Spiced Syrup

- 2 cups water

- 1 cup water

- 1 cinnamon stick

- 1 cardamom pod, cracked

- pinch of nutmeg

- 1 tsp vanilla

- 1-star anise

Cocktail

- ½ cup Kahlua (coffee liqueur)

- 1 cup chocolate vodka

- ½-1 cup spiced syrup to taste

Instructions:

1. Mix ingredients for syrup together in a saucepan over medium to high heat. Cook mixture until the sugar has dissolved, then remove it from the heat and let it cool. Once cooled, strain the spices out.

2. For the cocktail, mix the Kahlua, vodka, and syrup with some ice in a cocktail shaker and shake it until it is chilled. Pour the mixture into martini glasses.

3. Optionally, you can add a small pellet of dry ice into each glass and let it evaporate entirely before serving the drink.

Conclusion

Wizard, witch or non-magical folk - there is no excuse necessary when you need a magical hand in the kitchen. If you lack the skill, practice makes perfect. This book gives you the knowledge and teaches you the steps to put together powerful concoctions to impress any guest attending your incredible feasts and celebrations. The delicious configurations featured here are sure to take even your own mouth on a journey, not only through the wizarding world but also through British culture. From traditional to unconventional, nothing is left out.

Good luck, and happy cooking!

THE
POCKET
ROM-COM
MOVIES

Published in 2025
by Gemini Gift Books
Part of Gemini Books Group

Based in Woodbridge and London

Marine House, Tide Mill Way,
Woodbridge, Suffolk IP12 1AP
United Kingdom

www.geminibooks.com

Text and Design © 2025 Gemini Gift Books Ltd

Text by Roland Hall
Cover illustration by Natalie Foss

ISBN 978-1-80247-344-5

Manufacturer's EU Representative: Eurolink Compliance Limited,
25 Herbert Place, Dublin, D02 AY86, Republic of Ireland.
admin@eurolink-europe.ie

Printed in China

10 9 8 7 6 5 4 3 2 1

Picture Credits: Alamy Stock Photo: Moviestore Collection Ltd 4;
AJ Pics 6; RGR Collection 16, 118; Adobe Stock Photo: Vodoleyka 124,
125, 126, 127.

THE
POCKET

ROM-COM
MOVIES

G:

CONTENTS

INTRODUCTION

Rom-coms are like no other movies. They address a basic human need for emotion; we *love* them. They are fun, they are romantic, they are light, they are thoughtful, they are easy to watch and they (nearly always ... well, usually) have a happy ending.

Watching a rom-com is not a deep, meaningful activity. Or is it? There is nothing wrong with wanting to see regular people encountering the ups and downs of romance. After all, that is something that pretty much every adult on the planet can relate to, right? So rom-coms let us reflect on relationships from the comfort of a cinema seat or our home.

And more than that, they allow us to feel and express emotions: to laugh, to cry, to feel jeopardy and, once they are over, to feel better about the world – and there's nothing wrong with that, either!

Rom-coms have been around in one form or another for a long, long time. The classic story – boy meets girl, something goes wrong, something goes right, boy meets girl again, they live happily ever after – is one that's been told over and over again. But it is still entertaining, and there are still new ways of telling it.

"It's very hard to get a movie made these days that has a sad ending."

— Nora Ephron, interview with Kathryn Borel, *The Believer*, 2012

"Dating kind of has to be an act of reckless optimism, right? The triumph of hope over experience."

— Curtis Sittenfeld,
Romantic Comedy, 2023

And that is why rom-coms have survived – thrived – and evolved into their own hugely successful genre in cinema. They give us something that is at once familiar but at the same time different. We know there will be uncertainty. We know he/her/they will walk away at some point.

And we love it – because we also know that they will be back. That is not to say every rom-com is totally predictable, but it is to say that the genre's charm is about living the story, feeling the moments and enjoying the waves of emotions as they crash over us.

But what makes the best rom-coms?
Many things, for sure. They have the
funniest scenes, the saddest moments,
the most horrible characters, and the
nicest, too. The recipe keeps being
rewritten, and each new decade
brings us new locations, fresh
ideas, characters and moments to
remember forever.

This book lists 50 essential rom-coms,
chosen because they are outstanding.
Some are laugh-out-loud funny, some
are sad, but all of them are great –
and they will make you laugh, cry and
want to get out there and live...

"Those are the three big loves: family, romance and friends."

— Richard Curtis, interview with Katie Strick, *Evening Standard*, 2023

THE ROM FACTOR

There is a "rom factor" listed in the reviews that follow. It is simply an indicator of how weepy and romantic the film is, solely in the author's opinion.

A mark of 1 is given to a standard weepie with little jeopardy and a straightforward outcome, whereas a 5 indicates you will need an extra box of tissues while you watch. Enjoy!

"Human beings need other human beings."

— Nancy Meyers, interview with Hadley Freeman, the *Guardian*, 2015

★ ★ ★ ★ ★

50
MUST-SEE
ROM-COM
MOVIES

① Roman Holiday, 1953
Director: William Wyler
Runtime: 118 mins
Rom factor: 3/5

This is the grandmother of rom-coms, and definitely an essential watch, especially if you are unaware of the stunning talent that is Audrey Hepburn. She plays Princess Ann (from an unnamed country), who is in Rome as part of her European tour. She meets American journalist Joe Bradley (the dashing Gregory Peck). He doesn't recognize her, but later agrees to sell an exclusive story (without her knowledge) to his editor. The interview turns into a sort-of date, and the two slowly fall in love, culminating in a kiss after a dip in the river while fighting to escape the princess's guard.

The movie is funny, touching and beautiful, with a cracking dialogue and performances that even 60 years later seem so natural and graceful. But is there a happy ending? You'll have to watch it to find out!

"I've never been alone with a man before, even with my dress on."

— **Princess Ann**

"That sex was the most fun I've ever had without laughing."

— Alvy

② Annie Hall, 1977
Director: Woody Allen
Runtime: 93 mins
Rom factor: 2/5

Stop me if you've heard this one before (from Woody Allen at least): anxious Jewish New Yorker (Alvy Singer, played by Allen) wonders what went wrong in his relationship (with Annie Hall, played by Diane Keaton). Sound familiar? Well this is the original and best, not only of Allen's self-reflective, analytical movies, but it is also a really funny, serious, silly, touching, human movie. Even New York City has a part to play in this black-and-white introspective extravaganza.

Critics and general public agreed. *Annie Hall* scooped four Academy Awards, including Best Movie, and countless others. It really put Woody Allen into the mainstream – some would argue it is his best ever – and issues of relationships, neurosis, loneliness and marriage are dealt with in a hilarious manner.

③ Gregory's Girl, 1981
Director: Bill Forsyth
Runtime: 91 mins
Rom factor: 3/5

Not your usual rom-com, that's for sure. *Gregory's Girl* tells the painful story of young Glasgow student Gregory (John Gordon Sinclair), who falls in love with the girl Dorothy (Dee Hepburn), who turns up at his football (soccer) team and is better than all the boys. He asks her on a date, and the ensuing evening is a lovely ode to the excruciating pain of youth. Gregory's magical night offers so much and delivers in spades. But will he end up with Dorothy, or Susan (Claire Grogan) – one of a string of girls he meets?

The unusual aspects include many of those director Bill Forsyth (*Local Hero*) was famous for: cheeky Scottish youths, surreal plot twists and careful visual elements. *Gregory's Girl* is an uplifting movie, and the seemingly endless night in Cumbernauld (not a frequently filmed location) is a joy to watch. The sequel *Gregory's Two Girls*, made 15 years later, did not catch on.

"Oh, that
Dorothy...
the hair,
the teeth
and the
smell."

— Gregory

④ Splash, 1984
Director: Ron Howard
Runtime: 111 mins
Rom factor: 3/5

Splash certainly has a unique selling point: the main character falls in love with a fish! (To be fair, that's not quite true, she's actually a mermaid.) As a young boy, Allen Bauer (Tom Hanks) falls into the sea and meets a young girl (Daryl Hannah), who turns out to be a mermaid. As you may imagine, the two meet again and the comedy stems from "Madison" (the human name the mermaid chooses) as she attempts to fit in. After a series of wacky adventures, the romance kicks in, and the couple decide to make a go of it, but as with many aspects of this film, it's not a very traditional approach.

Splash is great fun, pretty silly, but has a lovely, enduring romantic aspect at its heart. Definitely residing in the "not even faintly credible" section, it does actually manage to work as both comedy and romance.

"What you looking at? You never seen a guy who slept with a fish before?"

— Freddie

"I'm not a one-man woman. Bottom line."

— **Nola Darling**

⑤ She's Gotta Have It, 1986

Director: Spike Lee
Runtime: 84 mins
Rom factor: 1/5

Spike Lee burst onto the movie scene with this hugely original film that challenged established tropes and narratives in what became a manner typical of the groundbreaking director. Nola Darling (Tracy Camilla Johns) dates three men and is happy with the situation. However, it turns out that they aren't, after the three get together and compare notes. After much discussion and some unpleasantness, Nola chooses one to settle down with. However, in true Spike Lee fashion, everything is not what it seems.

A clever, political movie, *She's Gotta Have It* uses racial and sexual stereotypes, and knocks them down in a provocative yet thoughtful manner. This is one for reflection rather than tears.

⑥ Moonstruck, 1987
Director: Norman Jewison
Runtime: 102 mins
Rom factor: 3/5

Moonstruck is a classic rom-com, falling into the "woman meets boyfriend's best friend/brother and falls in love with him instead" category. It works perfectly.

Loretta (Cher) and her boyfriend Johnny (Danny Aiello) agree to get married, but Johnny's estranged brother Ronnie (Nicholas Cage) must be invited to the wedding ... you can see where this is heading. What makes *Moonstruck* different is the strong Italian-American family background, which also adds a superstitious element, as reflected in the title.

Despite a few oddities that grate slightly with a modern audience (extra-marital affairs, stereotyping), *Moonstruck* is a great movie, and highlights Cher's versatile acting ability.

"Ma, I love him awful!"

— Loretta

⑦ When Harry Met Sally..., 1989
Director: Rob Reiner
Runtime: 95 mins
Rom factor: 5/5

When Harry Met Sally... has become the yardstick, the ultimate rom-com, the one by which all others are judged. And there's a reason for that. Expert direction from an established hand in the business, superb performances from the leads (believable vulnerability from Meg Ryan, underwhelmed indifference from Billy Crystal) and a brilliant storyline that spans more than a decade (written by Nora Ephron).

In case you missed it, Harry (Crystal) and Sally (Ryan) car-share back to New York following graduation. As they discuss relationships, their contrasting viewpoints quickly become apparent. After parting, they keep encountering each other over a 12-year period, realizing different things every time. The icing on the ultimate rom-com cake is the cut scenes, featuring (real life) dialogue from couples; Nora Ephron you are a genius.

"I'll have what she's having."

— Woman in diner
(Rob Reiner's mother!)

⑧ Ghost, 1990
Director: Jerry Zucker
Runtime: 127 mins
Rom factor: 5/5

This weepie pairs Hollywood heavyweights
Patrick Swayze (Sam) and Demi Moore
(Molly) as a New York couple very much in
love. The uncertainty in this rom-com comes
from nontraditional sources, as Sam is killed
in the very first scene. What ensues is a story
of murder, betrayal and – above all – love
that endures past the end of life.

It features one of the most famous scenes
in modern cinema, involving Molly and
Sam making a pot on a potter's wheel in
the middle of the night to the sound of the
Righteous Brothers' 'Unchained Melody'.
Who'd have thought clay could be such fun?
It is a hugely moving scene, and well placed
in the film, which is not so much a tearjerker
as a tear-extractor. Bring tissues ... bring a lot
of tissues.

"The love inside, you take it with you."

— Sam

"I want the fairy tale."

— **Vivian**

⑨ Pretty Woman, 1990
Director: Garry Marshall
Runtime: 119 mins
Rom factor: 4/5

Edward (Richard Gere) meets call girl Vivian (Julia Roberts). They agree for her to act as his girlfriend for a week in exchange for payment. Suffice to say, it doesn't go as planned, and feelings develop between prostitute and John. Hey, it was (only just) the '90s, and things were different then.

If you ignore that *Pretty Woman* has a few issues (not least the "prostitute straightens up for her man" theme), it is actually a very interesting film. Themes of empowerment, choice and equality are subtly hidden in this rags-to-riches story.

The public had no issues at all: *Pretty Woman* is still the No. 1 box-office rom-com in the USA with 41 million ticket sales.

⑩ Groundhog Day, 1993
Director: Harold Ramis
Runtime: 101 mins
Rom factor: 4/5

Bill Murray has played grumpy (old) men seemingly his entire career and *Groundhog Day* proves no exception. Phil Connors (Murray), a TV weatherman, is sent on assignment to Punxsutawney (try spelling that if you don't come from there), where the famous groundhog is due, signalling six more weeks of winter if he sees his shadow. Phil ends up living the same day over and over, going through many phases before he eventually becomes a decent person – and is released from the spell.

Groundhog Day is really funny, touching and very sweet. And although Andie MacDowell has only a supporting role, the chemistry between the two drives the film forward to its logical conclusion.

One thing's for sure: you'll never listen to Sonny & Cher's 'I Got You Babe' the same way ever again.

"I'll give you a winter prediction: It's gonna be cold, it's gonna be grey, and it's gonna last you for the rest of your life."

— Phil

⑪ Sleepless in Seattle, 1993
Director: Nora Ephron
Runtime: 105 mins
Rom factor: 2/5

Following the success of *When Harry Met Sally...* Nora Ephron was rewarded with the chance to direct what turned out to be the next big rom-com, this time pairing Meg Ryan with Hollywood nice guy Tom Hanks. To say it was a success would be a vast understatement, for the movie went on to break box-office records.

Recently widowed architect Sam (Tom Hanks) moves to Seattle with his son Jonah (Ross Malinger). After a radio appearance in which Sam discusses how much he misses his wife, many women get in touch. Jonah vets these and decides Annie (Meg Ryan) – who did not even intend to send a letter – is "the One" for his dad. Odd in that the main couple spend almost all the movie apart, *Sleepless in Seattle* is brilliant nonetheless, demonstrating the power of great cinematic storytelling.

"Look,
Annie ... I love
you. But let's
leave that
out of this."

— Walter

"I assumed, since we slept together, that we would be getting married."

— Charles

⑫ Four Weddings and a Funeral, 1994

Director: Mike Newell
Runtime: 111 mins
Rom factor: 5/5

Part of the British invasion of the rom-com, *Four Weddings...* was a box-office triumph for various reasons – not least of them the sight of the dashing Hugh Grant carrying on with American belle Andie MacDowell. Cool Britannia was underway at the time and Brand Britain was making waves as this star-studded film hit screens worldwide.

Foppish, unreliable Brit Charles (Grant) meets American Carrie (MacDowell) at a wedding. They encounter each other again (and again), get married (not to each other), but eventually love's path runs true.

Typically, for a Richard Curtis-penned film, there is so much more going on, with friends, family and lovers galore. It is a beautifully rich story, highlighting the frailties of humankind, especially when it comes to feelings.

"Why should I listen to you anyway? You're a virgin who can't drive!"

— Tai

⑬ Clueless, 1995
Director: Amy Heckerling
Runtime: 97 mins
Rom factor: 2/5

A teen classic, *Clueless* is on the lighter side of rom-coms, albeit loosely based on the Jane Austen novel *Emma* (1815). It is set in high school, where student Cher (Alicia Silverstone) does her best to influence teachers and other students alike. Until she meets her stepbrother by marriage Josh (Paul Rudd in his first big-screen role), after which her life begins to change. But this being a rom-com, it doesn't all happen at once.

Clueless is fun, frothy and very entertaining, featuring an enthusiastic cast hamming it up with wealthy West-Coast chic. It does have more depth than may appear at first sight, and the "be nice" message comes off as sincere. Director Heckerling's breakout film was *Fast Times at Ridgemont High* (1982), a different sort of high-school movie.

⑭ While You Were Sleeping, 1995
Director: Jon Turteltaub
Runtime: 103 mins
Rom factor: 4/5

An odd, basic premise drives the events of this classic weepie: Lucy (Sandra Bullock) works for the Chicago Transit Authority, where she has fallen in love with a commuter, Peter (Peter Gallagher) from afar. She saves him from muggers, but he falls into a coma. Claiming to his large, friendly family that she is his fiancée, her lies get out of control until she meets Peter's brother Jack (Bill Pullman) and they (both) fall in love.

A story about love, loss, family and friendship, *While You Were Sleeping* has the humour and humanity that is very hard to capture so well on the big screen. The wedding scene near the end is a classic, with suprises and shocks.

"Life doesn't always turn out the way you plan."

— Lucy

⑮ One Fine Day, 1996
Director: Michael Hoffman
Runtime: 108 mins
Rom factor: 4/5

If you put George Clooney and Michelle Pfeiffer together in a film, a rom-com would not necessarily be the first choice. However, the power of the two makes this a great movie. Both single parents and dealing with associated issues, Melanie and Jack (Pfeiffer and Clooney) are forced to work together to juggle their children, who go to the same school, with work commitments.

Shenanigans ensue, and serious questions are raised about family, future, employment and parenting, but eventually the couple become a couple. It's a nice movie, combining the frantic pace of working in New York City with the (seemingly) more sedate pastime of raising children. Two fine actors at their best.

"Jack, don't be a shit-head. Go rescue our kids."

— Melanie

"You complete me."

— Jerry Maguire

⑯ Jerry Maguire, 1996
Director: Cameron Crowe
Runtime: 139 mins
Rom factor: 2/5

Cameron Crowe both wrote and directed this movie, which digs into the world of sports representation – not famous for being a rom-com subject in itself. However, the relationship between the two protagonists, newly independent (i.e. sacked) agent Jerry Maguire (Tom Cruise) and the single mother who departs the big agency with him (Renée Zellweger as Dorothy Boyd) is such that the subject matter is almost immaterial. What is important is relationships, for that is what this film is all about: Jerry and Dorothy; Dorothy's son and Jerry; Jerry and his sole client Rod Tidwell (Cuba Gooding Jr, who won an Academy Award for the role).

Despite the lengthy journey, it is a touching, human movie, and the key scene "you had me at hello" has entered the annals of popular culture, with good reason.

⑰ As Good as It Gets, 1997

Director: James L. Brooks
Runtime: 139 mins
Rom factor: 3/5

Another film that qualifies in the "not-your-normal-rom-com" category, *As Good as It Gets* is a fascinating look at relationships. It's certainly a rom-com that is funny (very) and romantically themed (a bit less so), but there is a certain depth – not to mention sadness – about some of the characters that gives it a more heavyweight status than one would normally associate with rom-coms.

Heavyweights Jack Nicholson and Helen Hunt star as – respectively – Mervyn Udall, a grouchy OCD novelist, and Carol Connelly, the only waitress able to tolerate him. When she needs to move away to care for her son, Melvyn steps in to help. After many ups and downs, involving a number of interesting co-stars, the pair get together, but it doesn't seem to be a match made in heaven!

"Brace yourself for Melvyn."

— *As Good as It Gets* movie poster

⑱ My Best Friend's Wedding, 1997
Director: P. J. Hogan
Runtime: 104 mins
Rom factor: 2/5

An interesting diversion from the usual, *My Best Friend's Wedding* is a masterclass from Julia Roberts, who plays the longing best friend part to perfection. When Jules Potter's (Roberts) male bestie Michael (Dermot Mulroney) announces his impending marriage to Kimmy (Cameron Diaz), she swears to herself to do all she can to break them up because she's always loved him – and she certainly delivers on that promise. A series of lies, deceit and intrigue later, the path of true love is shown to not always run straight to the door of the female lead.

Featuring many notable scenes – 'Say A Little Prayer for Me' lunch, anyone? – *My Best Friend's Wedding* is a glowing example of the best rom-coms, from what was undoubtedly one of the golden eras of the genre.

"He's got you on a pedestal and me in his arms."

— Kimmy

⑲ The Wedding Singer, 1998
Director: Frank Coraci
Runtime: 96 mins
Rom factor: 4/5

One of the all-time great Adam Sandler vehicles, *The Wedding Singer* is a meta-trip around relationships and marriage (the wedding singer promises to sing at a new friend's wedding; is unable to sing at his own wedding; ends up singing at his own other wedding to previously mentioned friend).

Robbie Hart (Adam Sandler) is jilted at the altar (always a good start in a rom-com) and forms a relationship with Julia Sullivan (Drew Barrymore), who is engaged to another. The expected series of miscommunications, lies and cheating ensue, alongside plenty of singing. Most notable weepie takes place on a jet full of people travelling to Vegas.

Sandler and Barrymore play their parts to perfection, both coming across as genuine and likeable.

"Even Billy Idol gets it, I don't know why she doesn't get it?"

— Robbie Hart

"I wanted it to be you. I wanted it to be you so badly."

— Kathleen

⑳ You've Got Mail, 1998
Director: Nora Ephron
Runtime: 119 mins
Rom factor: 4/5

Nora Ephron weaves her magic once again in this lovely rom-com, based loosely (inspired, officially) on the delightful black-and-white classic *The Shop Around the Corner* from 1940, itself taken from a Hungarian theatre piece, *Parfumerie*. Whatever the origin, the story works perfectly.

Kathleen Kelly (Meg Ryan) runs a charming bookshop (called The Shop Around the Corner no less), which is under threat of closure when major chain Fox Books decides to open up close by. Joe Fox (Tom Hanks) is overseeing the new store. Unbeknown to each other, they are communicating anonymously online, where they get on very well but share no personal details at all.

They meet, dislike each other, meet again, dislike each other some more – on it goes until reaching the inevitable conclusion. But in Ephron's hands it works, really well.

"But mostly I hate the way I don't hate you. Not even close, not even a little bit, not even at all."

— Kat

㉑ 10 Things I Hate About You, 1999
Director: Gil Junger
Runtime: 97 mins
Rom factor: 5/5

Another teen movie (I'm trying hard not to use the word "romp") set in high school. What puts this one apart is the noble origin of the story, no less than William Shakespeare's *The Taming of the Shrew* (admittedly not the best of the Bard, seen through a post-#MeToo lens). However convoluted the story gets, at the core is the protagonist Cameron (Joseph Gordon-Levitt, a regular rom-com Romeo) and the object of his affection Bianca (Larisa Oleynik). Bianca's father has decreed that she may not date unless her older sister Kat (Julia Stiles) does, too. Patrick (Heath Ledger) is – literally – employed to do so, and off we go.

The young cast are obviously having fun, and there are many notable scenes, with Heath Ledger singing 'Can't Take My Eyes Off You' to an almost empty stadium, accompanied by the marching band, being one of them.

(22)
Notting Hill, 1999
Director: Roger Michell
Runtime: 124 mins
Rom factor: 3/5

Another great work from the pen of Richard Curtis, *Notting Hill*'s storyline may sound vaguely familiar, as a foppish Englishman gets romantically involved with an American. It is a case of the same but different, however, and with Julia Roberts playing a movie star, there is plenty of scope for blunders, mistakes and humorous faux pas all round.

Set, in – you guessed it – Notting Hill, London, William Thacker (Hugh Grant) shares an apartment with awful Welshman Spike (a genius cameo from Rhys Ifans). Who should walk into his bookshop one day but Hollywood megastar Anna Scott (Roberts) and the rest is – well – the rest is textbook rom-com.

Notting Hill is a really funny movie, even Roberts gets in on the laughs, though she doesn't make quite the impression that Grant does, showing his comic genius once again.

"You are lovelier this morning than you have ever been."

— Will

㉓ Runaway Bride, 1999
Director: Garry Marshall
Runtime: 116 mins
Rom factor: 3/5

Coming in at the tail end of the '90s, *Runaway Bride* pairs up two of the decade's biggest stars: Julia Roberts and Richard Gere.

The so-called runaway bride of the title, Maggie Carpenter (Roberts) finds herself the subject of a scathing newspaper article by columnist Ike Graham (Gere). Graham is sacked for inaccuracies in the story but later gets the chance to put things right by researching Maggie properly. He travels to her home town, to find that she is about to attempt marriage once more. The two bond, and you'll never guess the identity of the next man to be jilted at the altar.

In fact the film looks at ideas of marriage, control and autonomy in relationships, as well as self-knowledge – albeit in a light manner. The finale is bitter, the coda sweet.

"I know, in my heart, you're the only one for me."

— Ike

㉔ High Fidelity, 2000
Director: Stephen Frears
Runtime: 113 mins
Rom factor: 4/5

Moving the location of the source material may have been frowned upon by some, (Chicago being a world away from Holloway in London) but the core of the film – as in the book – is all about one man's self-knowledge and voyage of discovery. Record-shop owner Rob Gordon (John Cusack) is dumped by Laura (Iben Hjejle), causing him to reassess all his previous relationships and the reasons for their failures: it doesn't make for pretty viewing. Fortunately, Rob manages to work out what's what.

The rest is dressing, but what dressing it is: Jack Black clown cameos to perfection; the script cracks along; and there's more than enough vinyl-shop, muso nerdiness to claim "high fidelity" to Nick Hornby's original book.

"Did I listen to pop
music because
I was miserable?
Or was I miserable
because I listened
to pop music?"

— Rob Gordon

㉕ What Women Want, 2000

Director: Nancy Meyers
Runtime: 127 mins
Rom factor: 3/5

Starting the new century with a film containing an '80s throwback (Mel Gibson as chauvinist Nick Marshall) may seem odd, but that's not the oddest thing about *What Women Want*. After falling into a bathtub and electrocuting himself, advertising executive Nick finds himself able to hear women's thoughts. Is it a blessing or a curse? Given that his new boss Darcy (Helen Hunt) is a woman and that his estranged daughter (Ashley Johnson) has just moved in with him, let's hope it's the former.

Needless to say, Nick learns the error of his ways, but there's a fairly big trail of destruction in his wake. Fortunately, there are many ways he can make things right. It's silly, but great fun, and has some genuinely touching moments.

"If you know what women want, you can rule!"

— J. M. Perkins

"Bridget Jones, wanton sex goddess with a very bad man between her thighs... Mum... Hi..."

— Bridget Jones

26 Bridget Jones' Diary, 2001

Director: Sharon Maguire
Runtime: 93 mins
Rom factor: 5/5

Why did the producers feel it necessary to import an American to play a completely British character – the Bridget Jones of the title? Well it doesn't matter, because Renée Zellweger did such a fantastic job that it was hard to believe she is actually from Katy, Texas (and the actress was – deservedly – nominated for an Academy Award).

Working in a publishing house in London, Bridget is pursued by her boss, the caddish Daniel Cleaver (who else but Hugh Grant?). He messes her around (natch), and her parents try to set her up with do-gooder lawyer Mark Darcy (Colin Firth). You may spot the nods to Jane Austen's *Pride and Prejudice*. All does not go as planned. Bridget makes some life changes, and after a snow-bound run in her underwear (to 'Ain't No Mountain High Enough'), she lands the man of her dreams.

㉗ Serendipity, 2001
Director: Peter Chelsom
Runtime: 91 mins
Rom factor: 3/5

This film provides a reversal of the now well-established Brit male lead (usually Hugh Grant) and Yank female lead by casting John Cusack as the male interest and Kate Beckinsale opposite. It works.

Jonathan Grager (Cusack) meets Sara Thomas (Beckinsale) in a trendy New York department store while shopping at Christmas. There is an obvious attraction, which both of them try to deny or confirm in different ways. For various reasons, the experiment fails and they go their separate ways – for a few years at least. Picking up almost where they left off (i.e. not really getting together), both follow signs and symbols that ultimately – and I mean ultimately – lead them to each other.

It's a clever film, with plenty of cute twists and turns, and stellar performances.

"I first came in because of the name: Serendipity. It's one of my favourite words."

— **Sara Thomas**

㉘ The Wedding Planner, 2001

Director: Adam Shankman
Runtime: 104 mins
Rom factor: 2/5

As you might imagine, weddings are an eternally good subject for rom-coms. *The Wedding Planner* is no exception, as wedding planner Mary (Jennifer Lopez) falls for the fiancé of the person whose wedding she is arranging, the handsome pediatrician Steve (Matthew McConaughey). In a curious coincidence, he did happen to save her life. The film saunters around encounters between the two, their respective betrothed, families and an assortment of friends. The tension builds well throughout, and by the end you feel as if you've been talked from the edge by a caring relative – in a good way.

Maybe not one of the all-time Top 10 rom-coms, *The Wedding Planner* certainly packs plenty of charm into the minutes, and is well worth taking a look.

"His big day is her big problem."

— *The Wedding Planner*
movie poster

㉙ Two Weeks Notice, 2002
Director: Marc Lawrence
Runtime: 102 mins
Rom factor: 3/5

A shining example of the "opposites attract" rom-com subgenre, *Two Weeks Notice* pairs liberal lawyer Lucy Kelson (Sandra Bullock) with needy billionaire developer George Wade (Hugh Grant). He works knocking down and rebuilding; she specializes in historic preservation, but she ends up taking a job with him after he assures her he'll protect a community centre she loves. What could possibly go wrong? Plenty, as you might guess, and it is not long before Lucy quits (hence the title). But, surely, during those two weeks, anything could happen...

Two Weeks Notice is a great little movie, and the two leads are as excellent as you would imagine, sparking great chemistry between the two of them. No deep thought required, just a willingness to laugh and enjoy.

"I own the hotel, and I live there. My life is very much like Monopoly."

— George Wade

"There are two kinds of people: Greeks, and everyone else who wish they was Greek."

— Gus Portokalos

㉚ My Big Fat Greek Wedding, 2002

Director: Joel Zwick
Runtime: 95 mins
Rom factor: 2/5

A heartwarming rom-com that's big on tradition, family and acceptance, *My Big Fat Greek Wedding* is a joy to watch. Diving into the finer (and not-so-fine) points of Greek-American culture, the movie concerns Toula Portokalos, the daughter of Greek immigrants who run the restaurant Dancing Zorba's. She meets someone, decides to change her image, get educated and start dating, and eventually get married. The jeopardy concerns (mostly) her father's reservations and misgivings about her relationship with a non-Greek. By the end, differences are celebrated and all are happy...

Based on a true story, *My Big Fat Greek Wedding* was originally a one-woman show before it made it to the big screen. An independent smash, it made one-quarter of a billion dollars at box office.

"Girl, we are never gonna forget this honeymoon."

— Tom Leezak

㉛ Just Married, 2003
Director: Shawn Levy
Runtime: 95 mins
Rom factor: 3/5

On one end of the rom-com scale we have the artistic, with movies such as the multi-Academy Award winner *Annie Hall*. At the other end of the scale we find movies such as *Just Married*, a fun-but-forgettable jaunt around Europe with two newlyweds.

Odd couple – she's rich and he's not – Tom Leezak (Ashton Kutcher) and Sarah McNerney (Brittany Murphy) have just tied the knot and departed on their honeymoon. Unfortunately, each has a secret and they have not yet consummated the marriage. Much of the film is spent roaming around hotels trying to do so, with unfortunate results. It's funnier than it sounds, with plenty of laugh-out-loud scenes, and is ideal for a watching on a night in with friends, snacks and a drink or two.

㉜ How to Lose a Guy in 10 Days, 2003
Director: Donald Petrie
Runtime: 116 mins
Rom factor: 3/5

Mixing and matching means that it's the turn of Matthew McConaughey and Kate Hudson to pair up in a relatively jeopardy-free rom-com. The basic premise is an original one: he's an advertising executive, Benjamin Barry, who needs a woman to fall in love with him in order to win a bet. She's a writer, Andie Anderson, who wants to write a serious article about the differences between men and women ("How to Lose a Guy in 10 Days"). This is, obviously, a recipe for disaster, but a disaster played out across many amusing locations.

Hudson and McConaughey are superbly believable in their unbelievable roles, each adding just the right tone to the proceedings, and working the cracking script just right.

"Alright listen,
you can't name
my... my member
Princess Sophia."

— Ben

㉝ Love Actually, 2003

Director: Richard Curtis
Runtime: 135 mins
Rom factor: 4/5

Richard Curtis found himself in the driving seat for this star-studded spectacular, directing as well as writing. Ostensibly a film about love, it actually covers friendship, families, loneliness, longing, desire, mental health and more besides. It is long, but the hours fly past as the superbly intertwined characters navigate their way through the muddy waters of love.

There are too many great scenes to mention, but Hugh Grant (as the Prime Minister), wiggling his bum and dancing around Number 10 is certainly a highlight, and the obligatory chase scene at the end is lovely. Washed-up rockstar Billy Mack's (Bill Nighy) love story with his long suffering manager (Gregor Fisher) is touching, and the final scene is genuinely moving. Sometimes a film is more than just a series of stories, and this is one of them: *Love Actually* is love, actually.

"If you look for it, I've got a sneaky feeling you'll find that love actually is all around."

— David

㉞ Something's Gotta Give, 2003

Director: Nancy Meyers
Runtime: 128 mins
Rom factor: 3/5

Although not exactly famous for his rom-com roles, this is the second time Jack Nicholson appears in this list. This time he is paired with Diane Keaton who, like him, is a character finding love later in life.

The story involves Harry (Nicholson), a wealthy New Yorker with a habit of dating younger women. His latest squeeze has a mother closer to him in age, Erica (Diane Keaton), and the two eventually become close. Continents are crossed, lovers are spurned and arguments are had...

Where this film triumphs is in dealing sensitively and amusingly with couple's age differences and finding love at an older stage in life. Rather than being a hilarious cavorting romp, it's actually a pretty grown-up look at some difficult aspects of getting old and ways in which people deal with them.

"Erica, you are a woman to love."

— Harry Sanborn

"I think he's more than my friend. You're my boyfriend, right?"

— Lucy

㉟ 50 First Dates, 2004
Director: Peter Segal
Runtime: 99 mins
Rom factor: 3/5

Comparisons to *Groundhog Day* (see page 36) are to be expected, but *50 First Dates* is a different kettle of penguin altogether (you'll get it when you see the film). Adam Sandler plays Henry Roth, a marine veterinarian with a fear of commitment. Drew Barrymore is Lucy Whitmore, a teacher with a condition named anterograde amnesia, caused by a car accident, and which leads her to forget everything that happened the previous day. Sandler falls for her hook, line and walrus (again, when you see it), and the ensuing antics are a mixture of touching, gross and strange. It all adds up to a fairly undefinable film, but it is certainly worth a watch, and it's got a cracking soundtrack to complete the entertaining experience.

Sandler and Barrymore were to appear in another movie: *Blended*, in 2014.

㊱ Eternal Sunshine of the Spotless Mind, 2004

Director: Michel Gondry
Runtime: 108 mins
Rom factor: 4/5

It is not often that rom-coms go sci-fi, but when they do, the results can be spectacular. *Eternal Sunshine of the Spotless Mind* could be described as mind-melting, as the storyline involves the erasure of memories in a couple's relationship. Joel Barish (Jim Carrey) and Clementine Kruczynski (Kate Winslet) are a couple who have been together for two years; she decides to end it and have all memories erased. He does the same, but views them as they are wiped. It may sound complicated – it is – but it actually works incredibly well, with the stellar performances and bleak East Coast scenery contributing to the uneasy feeling, as someone else's relationship is unpicked before your very eyes.

Eternal Sunshine of the Spotless Mind is a brilliant watch. It is thought-provoking, surprising and fascinating.

"What a loss to
spend that much time
with someone, only
to find out that she's
a stranger."

— Joel Barish

"Life is not
the amount
of breaths
you take, it's
the moments
that take your
breath away."

— Hitch

㊲ Hitch, 2005
Director: Andy Tennant
Runtime: 118 mins
Rom factor: 2/5

In a slightly different premise for a rom-com, *Hitch* stars Will Smith in the title role (Alex "Hitch" Hitchens) as a man who coaches others in maintaining relationships (a "date doctor"). Now if this were a rom-com, he'd fall for someone unsuitable and all sorts of mayhem would ensue. Well it is a rom-com and that's just what happens, the object of his desire being gossip columnist Sara Melas (Eva Mendes).

Hitch does pose some interesting questions about relationships and what attracts people to one another, and it has a good message at heart. It's easy to identify the goodies and baddies, making it a fun, easy watch.

38 Failure to Launch, 2006
Director: Tom Dey
Runtime: 97 mins
Rom factor: 4/5

Although one made fairly subconsciously from the classic rom-com blueprint, *Failure to Launch* is still a classic. It features all the essential elements: man-boy who is unable to grow up (and move on); woman who is brought in to help him do so; friends/extras who disapprove of the situation; a couple who fall in love accidentally; a happy ending.

Sometimes there is nothing more to a rom-com than an hour and a half of laughs, a vague will-they-won't-they moment, and a joyful conclusion: we have a winner!

"I'm not afraid of love. I love love. Look, I've had a lot of girlfriends, right?"

— Tripp

㊴ The Break-Up, 2006
Director: Peyton Reed
Runtime: 105 mins
Rom factor: 2/5

This one forms part of a pattern of fairly low-key rom-coms that became prevalent in the early twenty-first century. Following a series of ever-more ludicrous scenarios, for a time the genre turned to more "normal" fare. *The Break-Up* is a prime example of this. Gary Grobowski (Vince Vaughn) meets Brooke Meyers (Jennifer Aniston), they fall in love and move in together. So far, so good. However, their relationship declines, eventually to the point that they are living together but separately. As you would imagine, it is a recipe for disaster, but it does make for some highly humorous scenes.

Vince Vaughn makes an all-too-believable slob, but it is still sad when the make-up leads to break-up. Jennifer Aniston can do no wrong in this bittersweet classic.

"Arrested for what, baby? For being awesome?"

— Lupus Grobowski

"Iris, if you
were a melody...
I used only the
good notes."

— Miles

㊵ The Holiday, 2006

Director: Nancy Meyers
Runtime: 136 mins
Rom factor: 3/5

Weighing in at over two hours, some might think *The Holiday* outstays its welcome more than some of the characters encountered in the movie itself, but in fact the time flies by. The cast is a curiously mixed bag of international talent. Amanda Woods (Cameron Diaz) falls for widowed single parent Graham Simpkins (Jude Law) in the English countryside. On the other side of the pond, Iris Simpkins (Kate Winslet) falls for Miles Dumont (Jack Black). This all occurs during a house swap the women arrange following miserable affairs of the heart.

Cultural differences are the source of many laughs, but there is a very tender side to the movie; all the characters are believable and, ultimately, vulnerable. If you have two hours plus to spare at Christmas, it's well worth it.

"I feel like I just found out my favourite love song was written about a sandwich."

— Jane

㊶ 27 Dresses, 2008

Director: Anne Fletcher
Runtime: 111 mins
Rom factor: 4/5

Another rom-com that draws on the traditions of marriage as its central tenet, *27 Dresses* is the story of Jane (Katherine Heigl), an almost professional bridesmaid who has accompanied her friends up the aisle (you guessed it) 27 times. One newspaper article and a handsome journalist (James Marsden) later, she's planning the wedding of her boss (Edward Burns), who she's secretly in love with, and her deceitful sister (Malin Åkerman).

Deceit in a rom-com means it's only a matter of time before someone is found out – preferably after a declaration of love that's unrequited. *27 Dresses* is a fun watch that isn't particularly deep or insightful, and it works all the better because of it.

㊷ Forgetting Sarah Marshall, 2008
Director: Nicholas Stoller
Runtime: 111 mins
Rom factor: 3/5

Forgetting Sarah Marshall is a rebound movie. Peter (Jason Segel) is in a relationship with famous actress Sarah (Marshall, played by Kristen Bell). She dumps him so he takes a vacation to Hawaii. Unfortunately for him (fortunately for the story though), Sarah just happens to be there, too, accompanied by her new boyfriend, the unlikely, unlikeable Aldous Snow (Russell Brand), a famous British rock star. Peter meets Rachel (Mila Kunis), who works in the hotel, and the kind of shenanigans you'd expect from a rom-com ensue. There are plenty of great laughs from the awful situations, and it doesn't all end happy ever after... or does it?

A cracking script – albeit very crude – and some cringe-worthy moments make this movie a brilliant way to spend an evening.

"…it kind of reminded me of a dark, gothic Neil Diamond. It's great."

— Aldous Snow

43 500 Days of Summer, 2009
Director: Marc Webb
Runtime: 95 mins
Rom factor: 3/5

As with *50 First Dates* (see page 87) and *Eternal Sunshine of the Spotless Mind* (see page 88), *500 Days of Summer* is a movie that plays with time. It is broken down into the 500 days of a relationship between Tom (Joseph Gordon-Levitt) and Summer (Zooey Deschanel), colleagues at a greetings card company. Their relationship arc moves up, then – unfortunately – down, before both of them move on, in their own ways.

This is definitely a movie to make you think (not least about the narrative as you try to piece together the story), but also about the nature of love, commitment, relationships and timing. It's very much a cerebral challenge, but really well made, and with a superb cast and script to boot.

"People don't realize this, but loneliness is underrated."

— Tom

㊹ He's Just Not That Into You, 2009
Director: Ken Kwapis
Runtime: 129 mins
Rom factor: 4/5

What do you get if you mix a self-help book, an all-star cast and a mixed bag of relationships? The answer is *He's Just Not That Into You*, of course. It's a long movie with a lot of characters, all of whom are trying to navigate the difficult channels of love, desire and commitment. If it sounds familiar, that's because it is. There's nothing particularly groundbreaking (or even heartbreaking to be honest) here, but there is a superb cast of talented actors that all contribute to a convoluted, widely spread storyline with affairs of the heart at its, um, heart.

It didn't rewrite the rom-com genre, but *He's Just Not That Into You* is a highly entertaining, diverting and thought-provoking movie.

"If a guy doesn't call you, he doesn't want to call you."

— Alex

"Margaret, marry me, because I'd like to date you."

— Andrew

㊺ The Proposal, 2009
Director: Anne Fletcher
Runtime: 108 mins
Rom factor: 2/5

For some reason rom-com writers like a publisher. Booksellers, editors and newspaper columnists are favourite occupations. In *The Proposal*, Margaret Tate (Sandra Bullock) is a pushy and disliked editor-in-chief at a publishing firm. She is Canadian, and it turns out that she is on the verge of being deported. If she was married to an American she'd be able to stay... Fortunately, her long-suffering assistant Andrew Paxton (Ryan Reynolds), is single and she coerces him into agreeing to marry her. They arrange to tie the knot in the bosom of his wealthy family – including a cameo from Betty White as grandmother. High jinks ensue, with even the family dog playing a part...

The movie works because it is a combination of silly, moving and thought-provoking. Oh, and Bullock and Reynolds gel brilliantly.

㊻ Scott Pilgrim vs the World, 2010
Director: Edgar Wright
Runtime: 112 mins
Rom factor: 1/5

We've talked about a few rom-coms that are slightly far from the norm. This one is so far away that it's almost – almost – not a rom-com. Except it is. After all, what is a common romantic trope if it's not dealing with exes? Without going into detail (you'd only be put off), Scott Pilgrim (Michael Cera) decides to pursue Ramona (Mary Elizabeth Winstead), a woman he dreams about and then meets. It turns out that first he has to deal with her exes. By "deal with", I mean "fight". It is surreal – it is based on a fantastic graphic novel – and that description doesn't really do it justice.

So you'll just have to trust us on this one: *Scott Pilgrim vs the World* is well worth watching, just don't expect the usual rom-com ingredients. Or story. Or characters. Or outcome. But open your mind and you'll be in for a real treat.

"If you want something bad, you have to fight for it."

— Wallace Wells

"I will never stop trying. Because when you find the one... you never give up."

— Cal

㊼ Crazy, Stupid, Love, 2011
Director: Glenn Ficarra
Runtime: 118 mins
Rom factor: 3/5

This movie looks at relationships through the eyes of a recently separated man and his friends and family.

Steve Carell plays Cal Weaver, a man whose wife (Julianne Moore) decides on a divorce after she has an extra-marital affair. Cal moves out and starts to navigate single life, something he takes to rather well, eventually, after he meets womanizer Jacob (Ryan Gosling) in a bar. The usual confusion ensues, but *Crazy, Stupid, Love* never feels false – it's a movie with heart, albeit with a slightly bittersweet taste.

One thing that puts *Crazy, Stupid, Love* in the top realm of rom-coms is the brilliant cast, who really bring the characters to life. It's a slow-burning, thoughtful classic.

㊽ Crazy Rich Asians, 2018
Director: Jon M. Chu
Runtime: 127 mins
Rom factor: 3/5

You go for ages in your list without a rom-com that has "crazy" in the title and then two come along at once. To be fair, that's the only thing this movie has in common with *Crazy, Stupid, Love*. For *Crazy Rich Asians*, we are very much back on the comedy side of rom-com. Adapted from the bestselling novel by Kevin Kwan, this movie draws on many (realistic, as it turns out) stereotypes surrounding relationships in the Chinese-American community. Dating, families, heritage and "the old country" are the dominant themes in this riotous comedy that moves at a furious pace, with cracking one-liners and farcical situations aplenty.

Rachel (Constance Wu) and Nick (Henry Golding) travel to Singapore for a wedding. There, they encounter Nick's extremely wealthy family (including his domineering mother played by Michelle Yeoh). It's a recipe for disaster, and what a ride it turns out to be.

"God forbid we lose the ancient Chinese tradition of guilting your children."

— Astrid

"I wrote five letters, so don't go feeling too special."

— Lara Jean

㊾ To All the Boys I've Loved Before, 2018
Director: Susan Johnson
Runtime: 99 mins
Rom factor: 3/5

As we travel further into the new millennium, the way movies are distributed changes. *To All the Boys I've Loved Before* was released on streaming giant Netflix, to great acclaim. And, in true streaming giant style, its success led to two sequels (*To All the Boys: P.S. I Still Love You* and *To All the Boys: Always and Forever*) as well as a TV series: *XO, Kitty*.

The premise is simple, but far-reaching: Lara Jean (Lana Condor) has written letters to all her crushes, but never mailed them. Her "helpful" little sister Kitty (Anna Cathcart) does her the favour of sending them. You can imagine the rest...

Sub-themes of sisterhood and family pervade, making *To All the Boys I've Loved Before* quite a deep, thoughtful film.

50 Always Be My Maybe, 2019

Director: Nahnatchka Khan
Runtime: 102 mins
Rom factor: 4/5

Hot on the heels of *Crazy Rich Asians* (sort of), *Always Be My Maybe* is another view of romance through the lens of Asian-Americans, this time Vietnam and South Korea. Sasha (Ali Wong) and Marcus (Randall Park) are childhood friends who lose touch, then get back together after many years. So far, so normal for a rom-com, and that's pretty much it. Sometimes the best story is the simple one, and the "will they, won't they" of the pair is beautifully spun.

What makes this movie work so well is that it is a rom-com film first and an Asian-American movie second, so the emotional aspects work brilliantly and are built upon and added to by the cultural clashes (and celebrations). One word of warning: eat before you see it!

"The man who embraces his mediocre nothingness shines greater than any."

— **Keanu Reeves**

DIRECTING THE
LOVE

Richard Curtis (1956–)

Born in New Zealand, Curtis did not move to the UK until he was 11. He sure made up for lost time and ended up working on some of the most iconic movies in British film history. He was a screenwriter for *Four Weddings and a Funeral*, *Notting Hill* and *Love Actually* (which he also directed). His television writing credits include *Blackadder*, *Mr Bean* and *The Vicar of Dibley*, some of the funniest and most popular British TV shows ever.

Nora Ephron (1941–2012)

Her credentials as a rom-com supremo speak for themselves, but Ephron was a writer, director and journalist, too. She wrote (among many others) *When Harry Met Sally...*, *Sleepless in Seattle* and *You've Got Mail*, and she also directed the last two. In 1983, after divorcing her husband, she wrote the book *Heartburn*, the story of a woman whose husband cheats on her, which was turned into a movie starring Meryl Streep and Jack Nicholson. It was by no means her last foray into the complicated world of relationships.

Jon M. Chu (1979—)

Although he only directed one of the movies in this book, it's one of the big ones: *Crazy Rich Asians*, one of the most successful rom-coms of the 2000s. Jon M. Chu has become one of the modern powerhouses of Hollywood. After CRA, he directed the Lin-Manuel Miranda-penned musical *In the Heights*, before following up with the hugely successful *Wicked* and *Wicked: For Good*. His star is still rising!

"I hope you laugh, I hope you cry, I hope you feel everything."

— Jon M. Chu, interview with Steven Mackenzie, *Big Issue*, 2024

Nancy Meyers (1949–)

Starting out as a screenwriter, Meyers enjoyed success right off the bat, co-writing *Private Benjamin*, for which she received an Academy Award nomination. She also wrote (and produced) *Father of the Bride* and *Father of the Bride Part II*. The three films of hers that are included in this book are *What Women Want*, *Something's Gotta Give* and *The Holiday*. Meyers was both producer and director for all three, and writer for the last two. She has plenty of other rom-com credits to her name, including *It's Complicated*, *The Intern* and *Home Again*.

Garry Marshall (1934–2016)

A veteran screenwriter, director and producer, Marshall was involved in shows on the big and small screen in the USA and further afield for decades. He was a writer on *The Lucy Show* and *The Dick Van Dyke Show*, and created the iconic TV series *Happy Days*. He directed the rom-com smashes *Pretty Woman and Runaway Bride*.

Marc Lawrence (1959–)

Two Weeks Notice is the only Lawrence-directed movie in this book, but he also wrote and directed *Miss Congeniality* (2000), *Miss Congeniality 2: Armed and Fabulous* (2005) and *Music and Lyrics* (2007). His actors of choice are Sandra Bullock and Hugh Grant.

Anne Fletcher (1966–)

Originally a dancer, making it into several movies in the '90s, Fletcher turned to choreography, and later producing. It was only natural that her directing debut would be a dance movie: *Step Up* (2006). That was swiftly followed by *The Proposal* and *27 Dresses*, showing her to be a classic rom-com movie maker.

"The truth of it is, I've loved you since the first second I met you."

— Charles,
Four Weddings and a Funeral,
1994